Culture and the Real

What makes us the people we are? Culture evidently plays a part, but how large a part? Is culture alone the source of our identities? Some have argued that human nature is the foundation of culture, others that culture is the foundation of human identity. Catherine Belsey now calls for a more nuanced, relational account of what it is to be human, and in doing so puts forward a significant new theory of culture.

Culture and the Real explains with Professor Belsey's characteristic lucidity the views of recent theorists, including Jean-François Lyotard, Judith Butler and Slavoj Žižek, as well as their debt to the earlier work of Kant and Hegel, in order to take issue with their accounts of what it is to be human. To explore the human, she demonstrates, is to acknowledge the relationship between culture and what we don't know: not the familiar world picture presented to us by culture as 'reality', but the unsayable, or the strange region that lies beyond culture, which Lacan has called 'the real'. Culture, she argues, registers a sense of its own limits in ways more subtle than the theorists allow.

This volume builds on the insights of Belsey's influential *Critical Practice* to provide not only an accessible introduction to contemporary theories of what it is to be human, but also a major new contribution to current debates about culture. Taking examples from film and art, fiction and poetry, *Culture and the Real* is essential reading for those studying or working in cultural criticism within the fields of English, Cultural Studies, Film Studies and Art History.

Catherine Belsey is Distinguished Research Professor at the Centre for Critical and Cultural Theory, Cardiff University. Her books include *Critical Practice* (1980, 2___), ___ *Shakespeare and the Loss of Eden* (1999) and *Poststructuralism: A*

D1145448

IN THE SAME SERIES

Alternative Shakespeares ed. John Drakakis

Alternative Shakespeares: Volume 2 ed. Terence Hawkes

Critical Practice Catherine Belsey

Deconstruction: Theory and Practice Christopher Norris

Dialogue and Difference: English for the Nineties eds Peter Brooker
and Peter Humm

*The Empire Writes Back: Theory and Practice in Post-Colonial
Literature* Bill Ashcroft, Gareth Griffiths and Helen Tiffin

Fantasy: The Literature of Subversion Rosemary Jackson

Dialogism: Bakhtin and his World Michael Holquist

Formalism and Marxism Tony Bennett

Making a Difference: Feminist Literacy Criticism eds Gayle Green
and Coppélia Kahn

Metafiction: The Theory and Practice of Self-Conscious Fiction
Patricia Waugh

Narrative Fiction: Contemporary Poetics Shlomith Rimmon-Kenan

Orality and Literacy: The Technologizing of the World Walter J. Ong

The Politics of Postmodernism Linda Hutcheon

Post-Colonial Shakespeares eds Ania Loomba and Martin Orkin

Reading Television John Fiske and John Hartley

The Semiotics of Theatre and Drama Keir Elam

Sexual/Textual Politics: Feminist Literary Theory Toril Moi

Structuralism and Semiotics Terence Hawkes

Studying British Cultures: An Introduction ed. Susan Bassnett

Subculture: The Meaning of Style Dick Hebdige

Telling Stories: A Theoretical Analysis of Narrative Fiction Steven
Cohan and Linda M. Shires

Translation Studies Susan Bassnett

Catherine
Belsey

Culture and the Real

Theorizing Cultural Criticism

Routledge
Taylor & Francis Group

LONDON AND NEW YORK

First published 2005
by Routledge
2 Park Square, Milton Park, Abingdon, Oxon OX14 4RN

Simultaneously published in the USA and Canada
by Routledge
270 Madison Ave, New York, NY 10016

Routledge is an imprint of the Taylor & Francis Group

© 2005 Catherine Belsey

Typeset in Joanna and Scala Sans by
Florence Production Ltd, Stoodleigh, Devon
Printed and bound in Great Britain by
TJ International Ltd, Padstow, Cornwall

British Library Cataloguing in Publication Data
A catalogue record for this book is available from the British Library

Library of Congress Cataloging in Publication Data
Belsey, Catherine.
    Culture and the real / Catherine Belsey.
        p. cm. — (New accents)
      Includes bibliographical references and index.
    1. Culture. 2. Reality. I. Title. II. Series: New accents (Routledge)
    HM621.B44 2005
    306–dc22   2004009650

ISBN 0–415–25288–1 (hbk)
ISBN 0–415–25289–X (pbk)

For Andrew Richard – in due course

Contents

LIST OF ILLUSTRATIONS   viii
GENERAL EDITOR'S PREFACE   ix
PREFACE   xi
ACKNOWLEDGEMENTS   xvi

1   What's Real? Butler, Fish, Lyotard   1
2   Psychoanalysis Beyond Idealism: Hegel, Lacan, Freud   20
3   The Lacanian Real   38
4   Žižek Against Lacan   52
5   Culture's Magic Circle   64
6   Making Space: Perspective Vision and the Real   81
7   Desire and the Missing Viewer   100
8   The Real and the Sublime: Kant, Lyotard, Lacan   119
9   Sublime or Sublimation? Towards a Theory of Culture   139

FURTHER READING   157
NOTES   160
REFERENCES   163
INDEX   169

ILLUSTRATIONS

5.1 Monument to John Simson, d. 1697, St Mary's
    Church, Debenham, Suffolk (detail).   66
5.2 Vincent van Gogh, *A Pair of Shoes*, 1887. Baltimore
    Museum of Art.   73
6.1 Carlo Crivelli, *Annunciation*, 1486. National Gallery,
    London.   88
6.2 Canaletto, *The Upper Reaches of the Grand Canal*,
    about 1738. National Gallery, London.   97
7.1 Jan van Eyck, *The Arnolfini Double Portrait*, 1434.
    National Gallery, London.   104
7.2 Phiz, *The visit at the Brickmaker's*, 1853, from Charles
    Dickens, *Bleak House*. London.   109
7.3 Diego Velázquez, *Las Meninas*, 1656. Prado Museum,
    Madrid.   111
8.1 Marcel Duchamp, *L. H. O. O. Q.*, 1919. Philadelphia
    Museum of Art.   137
9.1 Rachel Whiteread, *House*, 1993.   151

GENERAL EDITOR'S PREFACE

No doubt a third General Editor's Preface to New Accents seems hard to justify. What is there left to say? Twenty-five years ago, the series began with a very clear purpose. Its major concern was the newly perplexed world of academic literary studies, where hectic monsters called 'Theory', 'Linguistics' and 'Politics' ranged. In particular, it aimed itself at those undergraduates or beginning postgraduate students who were either learning to come to terms with the new developments or were being sternly warned against them.

New Accents deliberately took sides. Thus the first Preface spoke darkly, in 1977, of 'a time of rapid and radical social change', of the 'erosion of the assumptions and presuppositions' central to the study of literature. 'Modes and categories inherited from the past', it announced, 'no longer seem to fit the reality experienced by a new generation'. The aim of each volume would be to 'encourage rather than resist the process of change' by combining nuts-and-bolts exposition of new ideas with clear and detailed explanation of related conceptual developments. If mystification (or downright demonization) was the enemy, lucidity (with a nod to the compromises inevitably at stake there) became a friend. If a 'distinctive discourse of the future' beckoned, we wanted at least to be able to understand it.

With the apocalypse duly noted, the second Preface proceeded piously to fret over the nature of whatever rough beast might stagger portentously from the rubble. 'How can we recognise or deal with the new?', it complained, reporting nevertheless the dismaying advance of 'a host of barely respectable activities for which we have no reassuring names' and promising a programme of wary surveillance at 'the boundaries of the precedented and at the limit of the thinkable'. Its conclusion, 'the unthinkable, after all, is that which covertly shapes our thoughts', may rank as a truism. But in so far as it offered some sort of useable purchase on a world of crumbling certainties, it is not to be blushed for.

In the circumstances, any subsequent, and surely final, effort can only modestly look back, marvelling that the series is still here, and not unreasonably congratulating itself on having provided an initial outlet for what turned, over the years, into some of the distinctive voices and topics in literary studies. But the volumes now re-presented have more than a mere historical interest. As their authors indicate, the issues they raised are still potent, the arguments with which they engaged are still disturbing. In short, we weren't wrong. Academic study did change rapidly and radically to match, even to help to generate, wide-reaching social changes. A new set of discourses was developed to negotiate those upheavals. Nor, as new additions to the series demonstrate, has the process ceased. In our deliquescent world, what was unthinkable inside and outside the academy all those years ago now seems regularly to come to pass.

Whether the New Accents volumes provided – and provide – adequate warning of, maps for, guides to or nudges in the direction of this new terrain is scarcely for me to say. Perhaps our best achievement lay in cultivating the sense that it was there. The only justification for a reluctant third attempt at a Preface is the belief that it still is.

TERENCE HAWKES

PREFACE

What do we mean by culture? How extensive is its terrain? Has culture any limits? Can it tell us anything important about ourselves? And what pleasures does it have to offer?

There was a time when all cultural phenomena were traceable to human nature. This foundational concept provided an effective bulwark against change: the new was doomed to fail because it was, by definition, contrary to human nature. A generation ago, cultural critics overthrew the tyranny of human nature, and put culture in its place.

Culture had the virtue of allowing for difference, acknowledging the diversity of cultural values and practices. But it rapidly came to occupy all the available space. Now it was culture that explained everything, specifying what existed, defining our identities, 'materializing' our bodies. Culture became foundational. A thoroughgoing attribution of primacy to ideas, to the cultural script, has installed a new kind of tyranny. This version of culture allows itself no limits, no alterity, no resistances to speak of – and no place for desire.

It was the nineteenth century that specialized in theories of everything, centred on a single determining cause: the economy, for example, or sex. . . . Since then, without necessarily abandoning their insights, we have reread these theories to develop more *relational* accounts of causation. Not just the economy, say, but the economy *in relation to* politics and ideology; not simply sex, but sex in relation to death, and each in relation to the conventions obtaining at any particular time.

In this book I propose that we understand culture in relation to the real. I have borrowed the term 'real' from Jacques Lacan to define what we don't know. The real is not reality, which is what we do know, the world picture that culture represents to us. By contrast, the real, as culture's defining difference, does not form part of our culturally acquired knowledge, but exercises its own, independent determinations even so.

In Martin Heidegger's view, language throws into relief the world of things, making visible separate entities, objects, colours, sounds. And in this sense, he claims, language constitutes the means by which 'a people's world historically arises for it'. I like this image of reality popping up as things are named. But at the same time, Heidegger observes, while it indicates what is sayable, language also brings the unsayable into the world (Heidegger 1971: 74). That unsayable, the shadow cast by the vertical images of things, demarcates – but does not try to delineate – the real.

The real might be very grand: the immensity of the cosmos, for instance. Or it might be quite small, but mysterious. Jacques Derrida records the unnerving experience of meeting the gaze of his cat when he was naked. We easily take cats as objects of our regard, but what do they make of us? Anything, or not much? What is it to be a cat looking at a human being (Derrida 2002)? We pose the question from our own place in culture, but it cannot be answered from there.

The real enlists speculation. As what lies beyond culture, it also escapes the cultural script, defying by this means its assumed supremacy. And it enlists desire. Culture itself, paradoxically, inscribes strangeness, alludes to the unsayable. I conceive of *Culture and the Real* as following on from *Critical Practice*, first published in 1980 (Belsey 2002a), in two main senses. First, there I saw reading as a relation between reader and text. Here I try to develop that account by theorizing the pleasure of the text (without confining myself to the case made by Roland Barthes in a work of that name). There I was concerned with the imaginary sovereignty conferred by the text; here I go on to develop an account of the desire the text enlists. Second, I no longer see any good reason to isolate written material. To put my case in *Culture and the Real*, I have drawn on examples from film and the visual arts, as well as literature.

The ideas that have so radically shifted the horizons of the humanities disciplines in the past half-century appeared in the first instance as theories of culture in general. Once Ferdinand de Saussure had begun to prise language away from any supposed anchorage in the things or ideas, it became apparent that the account of the world inscribed in the meanings we had learnt might be no more than a product of culture. The separate entities distinguished from each other by language owed more to the system of differences we took for granted than to any guaranteed, independent existence.

If so, if, in other words, culture subsists as the meanings in circulation at a specific moment, the relations between separate genres or cultural forms might be as illuminating as the distinctions between them. In consequence, most discussions of culture are perceptibly moving towards cultural criticism, acknowledging the possible relationships between visual imagery and verbal constructs, without effacing the generic differences between them. English is spilling over into the terrain of cultural studies, cultural history into the history of art and architecture. In the interests of furthering these welcome developments, I here consider the relations between the real and spatial forms, as well as written fiction, without assuming a radical dividing line between media or, indeed, between popular and canonical culture.

One attraction of the New Accents series is that the books that constitute it have never been content with bland exposition. Taking nothing for granted, and committed to lucid explanation of the views they endorse or oppose, they have nevertheless represented interventions, not surveys. I have always found exposition for its own sake boring to read and to write. Instead, this book sets out to bring together elements derived from Lacan in conjunction with Jean-François Lyotard to constitute a theory of culture. As far as I know, this case has not been made before.

I do what I can to clarify the issues, counting on no prior knowledge of the debates. Poststructuralist theory is difficult for three reasons. First, a genuinely new argument is by definition unfamiliar, and needs unfamiliar terms and formulations to avoid sliding back into repetition of the old positions. Second, although on these grounds I would defend poststructuralism with my dying breath against accusations of jargon or obscurantism, we do well to remember that much of this theory emerged in the post-war era of high modernism, when any text that was readily intelligible looked like the work of a journalist. Third, poststructuralist writing may be highly allusive. It takes for granted a range of reference not available to many of us. Lacan, in particular, read voraciously and omnivorously, and this reading exerted a major influence on his thinking. He does not always acknowledge his sources in a conventional way. Much of the time he expects his audience of psychoanalysts to recognize his allusions without being told.

I have done my best not to betray the theorists I admire, though some slippage is inevitable in any paraphrase. I have also tried to present as accurately as I can the work of theorists I disagree with, especially Judith Butler and Slavoj Žižek. I hope they will forgive me if I have misunderstood them despite my best efforts.

Earlier drafts of parts of the argument have appeared in *Textual Practice*, *Symbolism*, *Études Anglaises* and *Critical Zone*, but I have revised them here, sometimes quite radically, as components of a continuing case. Many books in our busy, postmodern epoch are effectively collections of linked essays. By contrast, I have wanted in *Culture and the Real* to unfold a single, sustained narrative.

In the course of writing I have accumulated a great many debts. I am especially grateful to Charles Shepherdson, who knows a great deal about Lacan, Andrew Belsey, who is a proper philosopher, and Derek Hughes, who does wonders with Latin and Greek. Jean-Jacques Lecercle gave me a reading of Crivelli; Ailbhe Thunder checked up on the Grand Canal. Neil Badmington and I pooled our anxieties, as well as ideas and texts. My Cardiff colleagues generously provided research time, and Richard Whipp arranged it all. In addition, I owe specific valuable instances, stimulating ideas, useful information and helpful references to Elaine Brennan, Jana Lee Cherneski, Peter Coss, Dale Duddridge, Geoffrey Fisher, Martin Kayman, Christa Knellwolf, Pamela McCallum, Hugh Mellor, Jane Moore, Stephen

Ross, Susanna Rostas, Yoko Takakuwa, Julia Thomas, Louise Tucker, Keir Waddington, Garthine Walker, the Faculty of Arts at the University of Calgary, and the staff and students of the English Department, University of Regensburg. The General Editor, Terence Hawkes, has remorselessly exposed and corrected obscurity – in the nicest possible way.

Acknowledgements

The author and publishers wish to thank the following for their permission to reproduce images from their collections:

Photograph of John Simson's tomb is by Andrew Belsey.

Vincent van Gogh, *A Pair of Shoes* (Paris, summer 1887) courtesy of akg-images.

Carlo Crivelli, *Annunciation* (1486) © National Gallery, London.

Canaletto, *The Upper Reaches of the Grand Canal* © National Gallery, London.

Jan van Eyck, *The Arnolfini Double Portrait* © National Gallery, London.

Illustration from first edition of *Bleak House* (1853) courtesy of Cardiff University Library.

Diego Velázquez, *Las Meninas* © Museo Nacional del Prado, Spain.

Marcel Duchamp, *L. H. O. O. Q.* (1919) © succession Marcel Duchamp/ ADAGP, Paris and DACS, London 2004.

Photo of Rachel Whiteread's *House* sculpture by Nick Turpin © Independent Newspapers.

1

WHAT'S REAL?

Butler, Fish, Lyotard

THE PURPLE ROSE OF CAIRO

I can date very precisely the moment in 1985 when I first recognized the specificity of the postmodern. My sympathies were fully enlisted by Cecilia, the downtrodden wife at the centre of Woody Allen's film *The Purple Rose of Cairo*. I was relishing her pleasure in the black-and-white adventure story showing at her local picture house, when to my astonishment and delight, as well as hers, Tom Baxter, the romantic lead in the movie she was watching, came down off the screen to join Cecilia in the audience.

Much of the film is taken up with the fictional Tom's difficulties in the 'real' world. His money is movie money and restaurants won't accept it; violence, he finds out for the first time, can be painful; when he kisses Cecilia, he waits in vain for the fade-out and is not sure what to do next. He is not, Cecilia at last reluctantly acknowledges, *real*. But he is not simply Cecilia's fantasy either. The other black-and-white characters argue about how their film can go on without him, begging the projectionist not to switch it off and extinguish them; one presses her nose against the glass wall of the screen, complaining that she cannot get out. The actor who plays Tom arrives to coax him back where he belongs, on the other side of the screen, for fear the way-ward behaviour of his character will damage the actor's career. Inside the imaginary world of Woody Allen's movie, the comedy depends on a story that crosses the common-sense dividing line between fact and fiction. This is the line actualized by the presence of the screen itself, 'behind' which, as it naively seems, fictional characters conduct their thrilling, passionate or tragic lives, oblivious of the audience who have paid to watch them do so.

WALTER MITTY

There was a time when Hollywood knew the difference between fact and fiction, the story's 'reality' and dreams. In 1947, for example, Danny Kaye charmed cinema audiences as Walter Mitty, the irrepres-sible day-dreamer, who escapes from suburban life and an overbear-ing mother into fantasies, where he plays the hero of a succession of narratives derived from the pulp fiction he proofreads in his day-job. His imagined roles include Mitty the Kid, the fastest gun in the West, and Gayelord Mitty, the Mississippi gentleman-gambler, but my own personal favourite is Wing Commander Mitty of the RAF, in leather helmet and goggles, all self-deprecating heroics and right-ohs, his jaw a grim straight line as he brings down another Messerschmitt (*The Secret Life of Walter Mitty*, dir. Norman Z. McLeod). Walter's fantasies are clearly marked, in accordance with Hollywood convention, by a series of dissolves.

With hindsight, we might want to deconstruct this apparent antithe-sis between imagination and reality.[1] In 'real' life, the shy, unassum-ing Walter Mitty gets involved in an adventure concerning an heiress and looted jewels, and reluctantly becomes the hero of yet another pulp genre. Oddly enough, the romantic heroine has already featured in his fantasies before he meets her, so that Walter reacts with a double-take when he sees her for the first time in reality. And the bor-ing events which provoke the make-believe – his mother's endless shopping lists, a bridge game – also reappear in it, though transformed by their glamorous context.

But all this can easily be naturalized in a classic realist story: if Walter is genuinely caught up in a crime narrative where the villains include Boris Karloff, this only goes to show that life is stranger than fiction; true love, we know, always fulfils a prior dream; all fantasies reinterpret the everyday. The film is knowing about its own ironies, if in a softer way than the original short story by James Thurber.[2] Officially, the plot sets up a binary opposition between the actual and the imagined. On the surface, at least, we know what the story is asking us to take for real.

FICTION AND REALITY

In making this distinction, it confirms centuries of Western tradition: sanity, rationality, responsibility, the characteristics of the citizen entitled to play a part in society, and accountable before the law, are synonymous with the ability to tell the difference between reality and delusion. Only saints and psychopaths take their voices and visions for truth. The cinema screen that divides the brightly lit world of the fiction decisively from the audience in the darkened movie theatre marks that common-sense distinction between fact and fiction. *Fiction isn't real.*

Or rather, it wasn't. Our postmodern condition has made reality into an issue. What, we now ask, is real, and what a culturally induced illusion? Is there a difference between the two? Or is reality itself a product of our minds, either a subjective construct or the effect of culture? Recent cultural theory has contested the conventional view that human behaviour is predominantly natural, and that Western capitalist society in particular is the supreme realization of nature. Cultural criticism has successfully challenged the common-sense assumption that our social arrangements and values constitute the expression of a universal, foundational humanity. Indeed, we have also relativized common sense itself.

Ironically, however, this radicalism has been so influential (or, more likely, so fully a symptom of its cultural moment) that it has become fashionable to see human beings as entirely culturally constructed. Can we be sure, as Jean Baudrillard asks, where Disneyland ends and the 'real' America begins? Disneyland is part of American culture – but so is American culture. And Baudrillard concludes, 'it is Disneyland that is authentic here' (1988: 104).

In American theory, in particular, a thoroughgoing constructivism or culturalism is currently paramount. Historicism prevails in literary criticism. In the work of Stephen Greenblatt reality is understood to be synonymous with the cultural conception of reality, and this in turn is historically relative. For Judith Butler, whose work has so influenced thinking about gender, as well as for Stanley Fish in literary theory, culture is – or might as well be – all there is. From this point of view, while what we can know is entirely culturally relative, what exists becomes reducible, either explicitly or implicitly, to what can be *said* *to* exist. In other words, epistemology subsumes or occludes ontology.

POSTSTRUCTURALISM

European poststructuralism, by contrast, generally works harder. Starting from the insight of Ferdinand de Saussure that because words do not have exact equivalents from one language to another, meanings cannot be said to exist outside language itself, poststructuralist theory also affirms the relativity of what it is possible for us to know as subjects in and of the language we learn. At the same time, however, poststructuralism refuses to incorporate what exists into what we know exists, leaving open the possibility of a terrain of unmapped alterity which Jacques Lacan calls 'the real'. In contrast to the nonchalance of the culturalists, but without reverting to the foundationalism that has dominated Western thought since Plato, poststructuralism holds on to a structural uncertainty which I call 'the anxiety of the real'.

'The real', Jacques Lacan affirms, 'is what does not depend on my idea of it' (Fink 1995: 142). True to Saussure, Lacan makes a distinction between meaning, which we learn from language itself, and the world that language purports to describe. We have no evidence that the meanings we know match the world they seem to map. In consequence,

> One can only think of language as a network, a net over the entirety of things, over the totality of the real. It inscribes on the plane of the real this other plane, which we here call the plane of the symbolic.
>
> (Lacan 1988a: 262)

Truth, in consequence, is always an enigma. Lacan's real is not to be confused with reality, which is what we do know, because culture defines it for us. The real is what is there, but undefined, unaccountable, perhaps, within the frameworks of our knowledge. It is there as such, but not there-for-a-subject.

In Lacan's account, the meanings that give us our sense of reality are always acquired from outside. We learn to mean from other people, from a language that exists before we are born into it or, in Lacan's terms, from the irreducible Otherness of the symbolic order. As the subjects we become by means of our subjection to the symbolic order, we gain access to social reality, but we leave behind the real of the human organism in its continuity with its surroundings. From now on language will always come between us and direct contact with the real. But the loss will be made good in the end: we shall rejoin the real in death, which we can name, but not know. Death separates us decisively from subjectivity and its experience, including the experience of reality.

Because it cannot normally be brought within the symbolic order of language and culture, the real is there, but precisely *not* there-for-a-subject, not accessible to human beings who are *subject to* the intervention of language. Psychoanalysis, however, can bring to light the missed encounter with a real so unbearable that it cannot be named. Freud recounts the case of a father who, in Lacan's interpretation, woke up rather than continue to dream the appeal of his dead son, 'Father, can't you see I'm burning?' (Lacan 1979: 58–60). The dead child in this appalling ('atrocious') vision 'designates' a realm beyond reality, which is one of cruel loss (Lacan 1973a: 58). This loss is real, organic, but language cannot do it justice. Lacan comments that no one can say what it is to lose a child, unless the father *as* father, in the bond with his child that he cannot name as a conscious being in the symbolic order, in culture, in the reality we (think we) know. The dream comes close, but even there the real is evaded.

On the basis of this moment and others in Lacan's work, Slavoj Žižek constructs a philosophy of the real as absent, non-existent, seeing human beings as irreparably damaged by this absence. Žižek's traumatized people are at the mercy of a consequent social antagonism, which cannot be erased or wished away by dictators on the one hand, or well-meaning social democrats on the other. Žižek's political philosophy is original and persuasive, but ultimately it is not as consistent with psychoanalysis as he claims. I shall have more to say about Žižek in due course, but what matters for the moment is that Lacan's real, though not there-for-a-subject, lost, in other words, to the organism-in-culture that speaking beings become, continues to exist and will, in the end, reclaim us.

FICTION v. THEORY

By distinguishing between reality and the real, the known and the unknowable, poststructuralism acknowledges the relativity of what we can be sure of, without resorting to the position of the culturalists, who make what exists depend, in effect, on our idea of what exists. Recent cinema, oddly enough, shows more affinity with poststructuralism here than with the simpler world of academic theory. Since *The Purple Rose of Cairo*, any number of films have put exploratory pressure, in different ways and to varying degrees, on the fine line between illusion and reality.[3] Peter Greenaway's *The Baby of Mâcon* (1993) shows the action of the fictional play get out of hand, to the point where the actors in the play 'really' die. In *Pleasantville* (dir. Gary Ross, 1998) the crossover works the other way: two people from our present move through the television screen into the black-and-white world of a 1950s sitcom. Maurizio Nichetti's *The Icicle Thief* (*Ladri di Saponetti*, 1989) has modern commercials invading a television showing of the director's nostalgic monochrome tragedy set in the 1940s. The consequent slippage between parallel worlds leads to a happy and colourful consumerist ending for the fictional characters in the neo-realist, black-and-white film-within-the-film, while the director is caught behind the television screen, unable to get out. *Swimming Pool* (dir. François Ozon, 2003) unexpectedly prises apart fiction and the film's reality in the last reel. But when did the fiction begin, we are left to wonder, and how much of the action does it include?

The novel, too, has taken on some of these issues. Julian Barnes, for instance, plays confidently with the paradoxes of postmodernity. In *England, England* (1998) a tycoon buys the Isle of Wight off the south coast of England, and turns it into a theme-park 'England' for tourists. Not only does England, England, as the island is known, gradually displace England itself; unnervingly, the actors hired to impersonate the legendary icons of English culture begin to inhabit their roles, disrupting the smooth running of the commercial project in the process. The 'smugglers' start smuggling, to the detriment of the island economy; Dr Johnson falls into deep depression and ceases to entertain the tourists; and Robin Hood and his Merry Band refuse to obey the rules and outlaw themselves from the whole venture.

But since the visual juxtaposition of the imagined with what the fiction presents as reality is inevitably more scandalous, because more immediate, cinema always seems to have the edge. In *Last Action Hero* (dir. John McTiernan, 1993) Arnold Schwarzenegger plays Arnold Schwarzenegger playing the fictional Hollywood hero, Jack Slater. Jack crosses the line into the world of his own audience, where the bad guys can win. Gradually, the entire cast of fictional characters turns up in an actual New York, including the villains. Here Jack is in 'real' danger for the first time, when the fictional villains realize that if they kill Arnie, they will necessarily destroy the character he plays. But the fictitious Jack rescues the 'real' Arnold Schwarzenegger from assassination at the premiere of *Jack Slater IV*, and saves himself, as fictional character, from extinction.

Oddly enough, it is Jack who seems sympathetic: Arnold Schwarzenegger 'himself' is presented ironically as smug and insensitive, preoccupied by publicity and self-promotion. In an unexplained and distinctly uncanny moment, Jack tells the actor that he never liked him anyway: 'You've brought me nothing but pain.' Moreover, Jack is the one who looks 'real': Arnie, dressed up for the occasion, appears fake in the way that offstage actors often do.

In other words, these movies, including *Last Action Hero*, do not ask us to make the easy constructivist assumption that there is no difference between illusion and reality. Instead, they problematize that difference, call it into question, sometimes wittily, sometimes to disturbing effect. What should we make of this? Should we see these films as cinema at play, a sophisticated form of self-referentiality, postmodern metafiction? Probably. But that does not eliminate the possibility that it is also a cultural symptom, indicating an increasing uncertainty about the borderline between fiction and fact, between the lives we imagine and the simulacra we live, and a corresponding anxiety about the implications of that uncertainty.

THE 'UNCANNY'

Last Action Hero reaches a high point for me when Ian McKellen, as Death, comes out of the cinema where he has been appearing in Ingmar Bergman's film, *The Seventh Seal*, into the streets of New York City, but refuses to intervene on Jack's behalf and kill the villains, because he doesn't 'do ficshn'.[4] Six years later, in David Cronenberg's *eXistenZ* (1999) the distinction between fact and fiction has become in a more threatening way a matter of life and death. *eXistenZ* shows a group of people introduced to a new computer game, which is plugged into the body to achieve the maximum effect of virtual reality. After a series of hair-raising virtual adventures, including the virtual death of one of them, the participants step out of their game characters and discuss how far they enjoyed their roles. Suddenly, the central figures produce guns and kill the author of the game. Is this 'real', or virtual, we wonder. As they turn their weapons on another player, he begs, 'Tell me the truth. Are we still in the game?' And with that the movie ends. There is no way of knowing whether 'we' are still in the game.

The last reel of *eXistenZ* displays, no doubt knowingly, all the characteristics of the fully Freudian uncanny. Uncanny effects are often produced, Freud says, 'when the distinction between imagination and reality is effaced, as when something that we have hitherto regarded as imaginary appears before us in reality' (Freud 1985b: 367). The point about the uncanny in stories, where it occurs, Freud insists, much more commonly than in life, is that it depends on breaking the laws of genre. Supernatural events, he argues, are not in themselves uncanny: magic, apparitions, spectres and secret powers do not disturb us when they appear in fairy tales, where we expect them, or, for that matter, in Shakespeare. But their occurrence in what seems like realism, when the Gothic invades the mimetic, produces a degree of unease. The uncanny obscures the precise nature of the presuppositions on which the world of the fiction is based

(374). At the beginning of *eXistenZ* those presuppositions seem clear enough; by the end we have no way of telling whether the guns are real or virtual, and whether the damage they can inflict is final or merely for the duration of the game. But within the fiction the question is, in the full sense of the term, vital.

ANXIETY

For Freud the uncanny marks the return of the repressed or the culturally unsurmounted. Hollywood has often made capital out of the uncertain line between fiction and reality. The self-referential jokes of the Marx Brothers, or of Bob Hope and Bing Crosby in a succession of *Road* movies, indicate the comic potential of an appeal to the audience's knowledge that what they are watching is fiction, not reality. But these allusions invite us to feel *more* knowing, not less. By contrast, the films I have identified as postmodern promote uncertainty, a frisson of unease, as they call into question the presuppositions they seem to inscribe. Is it possible that this uncanny quality marks an unresolved cultural anxiety about our identity as subjects of culture?

Culture is the element we inhabit as speaking beings; it is what makes us subjects. Culture consists of a society's entire range of signifying practices – rituals, stories, forms of entertainment, lifestyles, sports, norms, beliefs, prohibitions and values. In our own globalized society it includes art and opera, fashion, film, television, travel and computer games. Culture resides in the meanings of those practices, the meanings we learn. The subject is what speaks, or, more precisely, what signifies, and subjects learn in culture to reproduce or to challenge the meanings inscribed in the signifying practices of the society that shapes them. If subjectivity is an effect of culture, of the inscription of culture in signifying practice, there is no place for human beings outside culture.

Culture, therefore, is all we know. In that sense, we are always in culture – always in the game. And if so, there is nothing we can be sure of, even when it's vital. Culture is what we know – or think we do. In practice, we can never be certain of it, because it is known in language (or in its equally symbolic surrogates, logical notation or mathematical equations). Knowledge exists at the level of the symbol, and there is no way of showing that any specific set of symbols maps the world accurately. Our mastery of the world depends on our ability to map it, to recognize the difference between fact and fiction, but we cannot do so with absolute confidence.

Is any anxiety we feel about the unknown real merely residual, a vestige of foundationalism in the postmodern condition, a longing to return to the tradition of Western thought since Plato, which insists on the distinction between appearance and reality? Are these metacinematic movies registering a change in that world picture, but grudgingly, harking back to an epoch that believed we could know when we were not in the game? Culturalists would say so. The theoretical assault on foundationalism has been so successful that it has produced its binary opposite, a thoroughgoing constructivism that celebrates culture as all-embracing. From this perspective there is only culture, and unease about this is pointless, merely nostalgic, literally *groundless*.

This culturalist insouciance seems to me inviting, but ultimately reductionist. If my anxiety remains in place, it does so not, I hasten to stress, as the prelude to an assault on the postmodern, and on poststructuralism as its philosophy, in the mode of Terry Eagleton and Christopher Norris. On the contrary, I don't want truth back. Whose truth was it, anyway? What I want to hold on to is my unease, on the grounds that the banishment of anxiety is not sanity, paradoxically, so much as psychosis. Genuine madness is being certain you're always in the game.

Conversely, if there is anything beyond the reach of our knowledge, not just for the moment, out of ignorance, but unknowable in principle, we can never be sure when we might reach the limits of the game, or when our cultural knowledges might fail us. If anything resists the sovereignty of the symbolic order, we always risk the uncanny possibility of an encounter that exceeds what culture permits us to define.

JUDITH BUTLER

In 1990 Judith Butler's book *Gender Trouble* electrified cultural critics all over the world. Butler's brilliant insight was that speech-act theory could be harnessed for feminism and queer studies to demonstrate the performativity of sexual identity. She countered essentialism and identity politics with sexuality as theatre, a display of 'corporeal style' (1999: 177), in which parody and the masquerade demonstrated the constructed character of gender as impersonation. Sexual disposition was not an origin but an effect of repeated social performances, none more 'natural' than any other. And just as gender is constituted by repeated acts, the idea of 'an essential sex' is culturally produced to mask gender's contingent character (180).

The conventional feminist distinction between biological sex and cultural gender was regressive, Butler argued, leading to a naturalization of gender characteristics rooted in the body. For her, by contrast, sex and gender were one and the same (10–11); what passed for nature in practice was a product of culture; nature was incorporated into culture. Butler's anti-foundational feminism, and her opposition to heterosexual hegemony, which I wholeheartedly share, are secured by overriding the anxiety about the limits of culture that I have suggested is evident in culture itself.

Her denaturalization of sexual identity brought Butler close to Michel Foucault, whose broadly poststructuralist work had historicized and thus relativized not only homophobia, but also homosexuality itself. This invested her position with a kind of familiarity which lent it authority. And Foucault in turn brought her close to poststructuralism. But the French tradition inherited a more complex account of the relation between the human organism and the culture in which it becomes a signifying subject. Much of *Gender Trouble* is therefore devoted to a critique of French psychoanalysis and Foucault himself, if in versions that it is sometimes hard to recognize. As Antony Easthope puts it, 'too often I feel that Butler's copy of Lacan is not the one I've been reading, but another by an author of the same name' (2002: 90). Oddly enough, however, in the Preface to the second edition of the book in 1999, Butler says that her theories were a 'cultural translation' of poststructuralism itself (1999: viii–ix). I can see no way of accounting for this claim.

Gender Trouble stressed the regulatory character of culture: heterosexuality was a discursive regime, and the possibilities for resistance were limited. But subversion could be read, in Butler's account, as a matter of choice, as if, because it was purely cultural, sexual identity could be improvised from moment to moment, 'enacted' at will:

> The culturally constructed body will then be liberated, neither to its 'natural' past, nor to its original pleasures, but to an open future of cultural possibilities.
>
> (Butler 1999: 119)

At such moments *Gender Trouble* sounds remarkably close to the American dream. In practice, norms are not so easily subverted, however, and this reading had to be corrected, along with the impression that physiology was reducible to mere discourse. Three years later, in *Bodies that Matter*, Butler insists on performativity rather than performance; the emphasis on theatricality is much reduced in the analysis (though it returns in the style of the writing); and the politics is less utopian, an issue of rearticulation and resignification.

Accordingly, in a rewriting of Foucault's '"reverse" discourse', where the identification of a group of people as 'deviant' paradoxically affords them a place to speak from (Foucault 1979: 101), she urges that words used as terms of abuse ('queer', for example) can be reappropriated with pride (Butler 1993: 223–42). Butler concedes a 'materiality' which accounts for the questions that properly concern the biological sciences, or for our ability to specify 'hormonal and chemical composition, illness, age, weight, metabolism, life and death' (66). Bodies are still 'produced' by culture, however, and sex is 'materialized' by regulatory norms, as the result of a process of 'forcible reiteration', the repetition of the cultural script (1–2). 'Sex' itself is to be construed 'no longer as a bodily given on which the construct of gender is artificially imposed, but as a cultural norm which governs the materialization of bodies' (2–3).

I am not at all sure how we are to understand the materialization of sex or bodies, but it is clear that there is no space in Butler's account for the anxieties that recur in popular cinema or poststructuralist theory about the limits of the cultural game. On the contrary, in her version of the story it has no limits. The question for Butler is not what exists, but what we know. What lies beyond this features in her theory only as a requirement on knowledge, a demand to be named, pressing to be theorized or explained in language. Anything that is not there-for-a-subject might as well not be there at all.

To secure her conflation of sex and gender, Judith Butler makes culture constitutive. Speech acts bring into being what they name, and 'Performativity is the discursive mode by which ontological effects are installed' (1994: 33; cf. 1993: 11). Culture, the inscription of meanings, modifies the materiality that motivates it. There is nothing that cannot be mapped in laguage, because for Butler language is ultimately referential. Materiality, in her intensely difficult prose, turns out to be the referent of language, and is approached through the signified, which it never fully escapes (1993: 68–9).

Seduced by the vocabulary of signifier and signified, we might easily miss the absence here of Saussure's altogether more modest account of signification. In Saussurean theory language is differential, not referential; the world is outside the sign, which is no longer the sign of something; the signified (meaning) offers no approach to a referent. This is not to say, of course, that meanings are not lived. But it does leave open the possibility of a domain of meaning-less alterity.

PSYCHOANALYSIS

According to Lacan's version of Freud, social reality offers gratifications, including sexual gratifications. But because language is irreducibly Other than the organism that we also are, the satisfactions available to the speaking being never quite match the wants they are intended to meet. When the little human animal becomes a symbolizing subject, something is left out of what language permits it to say. Its demands, in other words, belong to the alien language, not to the organism, and the gap between the two constitutes the location of unconscious desire. Desire, then, subsists in ways that are not culturally scripted, not the result of habit or the repetition of speech acts. Desire, unfortunately for us, is never quite 'performed' in our speech acts, but continues to make its disruptive presence felt in them for that very reason.

Psychoanalysis sees human beings as driven by determinations that bear a more complex relation to culture. The drives are psychic representatives of instincts. They thus participate in both culture and the real. The 'person' in psychoanalysis does not consist of ideas that materialize a body, and still less a mind *and* a body. Instead, we are speaking beings, divided between a real organism that inhabits an organic world and a subject that makes demands in symbols so irreducibly Other that they leave in place a memory of loss, which continues to insist as unconscious desire.

From this perspective, the real, culture's *difference*, without which the term has no meaning, is that silent or silenced exteriority which is also inside us, and which we cannot symbolize, delimit, specify or know, even when we can name it 'the real'. That term invests it with a substantial but remarkably indeterminate character. We shall, however, revert to the real in the end, in death. Death doesn't do fiction, but eliminates the body and the speaking subject, with all it thinks it knows. Death puts an end to the cultural game for each of us.

The real is not nature, the terrain that Western science has set out since the seventeenth century to map and master, and which Terry Eagleton invokes to counter culturalism in his book, *The Idea of Culture* (2000). Nor is the real a fact – of the kind bluff common sense might invoke to crush speculation. Still less is it the truth, a foundation on which to base new laws or dogmas, or an alternative reality with which to contrast appearances. On the contrary, the real is a question, not an answer.

Though the gods also belong to the real, it has nothing whatever to do with the supernatural, a realm devised to comfort or scare us, and variously explained or mystified by theologians and visionaries. Obstinately, brutally *there*, the real is not a content, nevertheless. What we don't know, individually or culturally, might be anything, or not much. Though it exists as a difference, there is no meaning in the real. Indifferent to description, it exceeds representation and brings language to an impasse. If we experience it, we do so as a gap, or alternatively as a limit, the point at which culture fails us. The real is what our knowledge, individually or collectively, both must and cannot accommodate.

STANLEY FISH

In 1989, a year before *Gender Trouble* appeared, Stanley Fish published a new collection of essays, one of which featured a character called 'rhetorical man'. This figure, who recognizes that the world is pervaded by language, is an actor who uses words both to manipulate reality and to fabricate himself; his identity is essentially histrionic, performative (Fish 1989: 471–502, esp. 483–4). Fish shares Butler's attribution of primacy to language, but his much more accessible prose throws the issues into clearer relief.

He explicitly rejects the Saussurean view that meaning resides in language, redefining this as the altogether improbable conviction that meaning is timeless, independent of context, and derived from mechanical features (4, 7). Fish's preferred alternative assigns meaning to ideas, in accordance with the tradition of Western idealism dating from the moment when Descartes identified being with thought in the 'I think' that proves 'I am'. Fish sees meaning as whatever the speaker has in mind. And since, as he acknowledges, we have no access to this, it follows that meaning must be purely contextual, a matter of what a member of a specific 'interpretive community' takes it to be in consequence of his or her conventionally induced beliefs. Truth and falsehood exist as relative terms, the effect of a specific point of view. Meanwhile, discursive change transforms the objects of knowledge, and the world of things comes into line with the world of ideas. An interpretive community represents a political grouping to the degree that it excludes dissent, since to disagree is to align oneself with another community. And so, in summary, 'all facts', as well as all values, 'are social and political constructs' (19–20, 26).

Since he avoids difficult questions about sex, Fish has no need to define a concept of 'materiality', and in consequence, he generally appears a more thoroughgoing cultural constructivist than Butler. On the other hand, since his theory is altogether less ambitious, he can occasionally allow for a distinction between what we know and what exists. Thus, in a discussion of the disputed historicity of a displaced African slave, Fish concedes, 'either Kunta Kinte was real or he was not'. But the point, from Fish's perspective, is not whether he existed or not. It is that the procedures for establishing what is real are conventional, and whatever these procedures produce will have the status of a fact (55–6).

CULTURAL DETERMINISM

Both Fish and Butler make large claims for the sovereignty of human culture over the world of things. Reality is more or less what we make it; material objects are shaped by language; identity is cultural and performative. But cultural determinism cuts both ways. If what we are is culturally scripted, we cannot be the source of our own beliefs, actions, selves. On the contrary, we are the helpless prod-ucts of determinations that exist in our communities. Fish affirms that we have no freedom of opinion, and that the only alternative views open to us are those of another interpretive community; Butler sees the sole way to influence change as repetition of the cultural script with a difference. Neither has grounds for confidence that things will change much, or that change will be for the better if they do.

Stanley Fish argues that if you want to resist, you have to move out and find another more sympathetic community. Judith Butler remains committed to resistance, but can see no adequate way of theorizing the possibility. The radical credentials of cultural construc-tivism do less than justice, it seems, to the distinctly liberal views of its main proponents.

THE REAL OF SEXUAL DIFFERENCE

In *The Truman Show* (dir. Peter Weir, 1998) Truman himself is the only person who does not know that he is the star of a television serial. Born on the set, Truman supposes that Seahaven, domed, climate-controlled, safe, socially predictable, is all there is. This leaves him at the mercy of a world he does not even know is scripted. But driven by dissatisfaction and desire, in front of a worldwide TV audience represented in the movie by characters whose consecu-tive responses to the show the camera makes familiar to us, Truman tries to leave town and travel. His efforts to escape are repeatedly frustrated, until he sails as far as the horizon and finds an exit button. The way out is a black rectangle against the plaster sky, the unknown, perhaps the void. *The Truman Show* juxtaposes the imaginary world of Seahaven with the reality of the audience watching the true man's struggles to escape the fiction he believes in, and with a third term, a black hole, the real.

The real provokes anxiety precisely to the degree that it is not ours to control. Fish brackets the real: it is not his concern. Butler denies its independence, but in doing so, in my view, she impoverishes the politics of gender. Sexual difference belongs to the real, to the extent that it generates anxiety *as* difference, while resisting symbolization. Sexual difference cannot be reduced to a distinction between this and that, or to decisive criteria for assigning bodies to one side or another of a single binary axis. Babies are not always born unequivocally male or female. Olympic athletes have to be classified before they can be entered for either men's or women's events, but no infallible test has yet been produced to settle the question in marginal cases. Sometimes the evidence of anatomy conflicts with that of hormones or chromosomes. No single indicator seems to be final.

Judith Butler's preferred term is 'sex', which points to an essence, and her case is designed to contest the appeal to the biological 'facts' of a single binary opposition as the ground of identity. But sexual difference is not an essence, and can hardly constitute a ground. Difference is a relationship, a space between things, not a thing in itself, not even a fact. And everything we know indicates that it is by no means binary.

Lived in history, of course, sexual difference remains a condition for cultural politics to reckon with, though not necessarily as a determining one, and certainly not as natural, where nature is viewed as either prescriptive or inert. What we make of sexual difference, whether as oppression or diversity, we make in culture. But it doesn't follow that we make it up, or that we can by means of performatives make away with it. The relation between the subject and the real organism that we also – and inextricably – are renders feminist and queer politics no less imperative: just more difficult, and therefore more demanding.

LYOTARD

In the text of a seminar first published in 1987, Jean-François Lyotard addresses the question, 'Can Thought Go On Without a Body?'. He concludes that it cannot, and not just because, if language constitutes the software of human thinking, the body provides the hardware without which this software cannot operate. We should recognize in addition, he claims, something specific about human thought-processes, including creative processes, which distinguishes them from the logical, binary, data-sorting, problem-solving efforts of memory performed by computers. Lyotard sees human thinking, by contrast, as analogical, lateral, intuitive, inventive. And this is so because we are *driven* to an uncomfortable, difficult engagement with what has not been thought previously, impelled by a force beyond pleasure, by a sense of 'lack': 'we think in a world of inscriptions already there. Call this culture if you like. And if we think, this is because there's still something missing in this plenitude' (Lyotard 1991: 20).

According to Lyotard, surely the most Lacanian of philosophers, culture itself is always lacking. And the paradigm instance of this insufficiency is sexual difference, the evidence that we are *all* empirically incomplete. Sexual difference entails something that each of us is not, does not know, cannot experience. Neither machines nor people can fully think this difference, let alone resolve it:

> Not only calculation, but even analogy cannot do away with the remainder left by this difference. This difference makes thought go on endlessly and won't allow itself to be thought.
>
> (Lyotard 1991: 23)

RESISTANCE

Sexual difference in Lyotard's argument is not the origin of thinking, but an instance of its condition, and to revert to Lacan's terms (as Lyotard himself is willing on other occasions to do), that condition is ultimately intelligible as culture's own unconscious awareness of the lost real. We might even want to say that the absence of the real is the motive for culture – and for the resistance to culture's regulatory norms. This motive is recurrently figured in Western thought as the darkness of Plato's cave, St Augustine's restlessness, fear in Hobbes, Freud's civilized discontent or Lacan's unconscious desire, the causes of change.

In Judith Butler's case, what looked at first like the dream of freedom turned out in practice to be a form of determinism. For Fish, culturalism presents a world that looks all too like Truman's Seahaven: safe, but repetitive. Cultural constructivism reckons without the real, however, and the something missing in culture itself which makes thought go on endlessly. The sense of an alterity beyond culture, pushing and pulling it out of shape, permits us to escape the cultural determinism and the cycle of repetition. Our relation to the world is capable of change: things can be other than they are. The gap between culture and the real is a cause of dissatisfaction which impels us to want more.

If so, current cultural theory confronts the question of the status and the limits of culture itself. On that depends our conception of human beings and their relation not only to the sexual possibilities, but also to the political obligations, of the world we inhabit.

2

PSYCHOANALYSIS BEYOND IDEALISM

Hegel, Lacan, Freud

TLÖN

In one of his most inventive and teasing fictions, Jorge Luis Borges describes a planet where the entire culture attributes primacy to ideas. Tlön has no things, and in its original form, the language had no nouns to name them. The people of Tlön do not practise science: in a world without objects, there are no laws of nature. On the contrary, in fact: reality owes its existence to the materialization of an idea. One school of thought on Tlön holds that the future is reducible to what people hope for, and the past no more than whatever they remember. In consequence, the past is just as malleable as the future. If archaeology names articles that would prove its own account of history, they are sure to turn up in due course. Conversely, ancient buildings begin to disintegrate as soon as there is no one left to remember them. The main intellectual discipline on Tlön is psychology; philosophy, meanwhile, is no more than a branch of the literature of fantasy.

WHAT EXISTS – AND WHAT DO WE KNOW ABOUT IT?

To admirers of Judith Butler and Stanley Fish, Tlön is not as absurd as we might think. The success of cultural constructivism depends on the subscription, increasingly widespread in Western culture at large, to a view our own planet's version of philosophy would define as *idealist*. Idealism, or the attribution of primacy to ideas, has a long history in Western thought as one way – not, in my view, a very satisfactory one – of dealing with questions about what we know and what exists.

It is easy to assume that what we don't know does not exist. To all intents and purposes, it doesn't – until it imposes limitations on what we can do. When the apple fell from the tree he was sitting under, Isaac Newton explained the event in terms of the law of gravity, but to this day, scientists don't know what causes gravity. This does not mean that they can jump off the Eiffel Tower with impunity, however. Medieval sailors may well have believed the world was flat. But even if they did, they would not have been able to steer their ships off the edge of it. For centuries smokers did not know that tobacco could cause lung cancer. That didn't make them immune to it.

The relation between what exists and what we know presents a philosophical puzzle. The problem becomes acute in the light of our inclination to identify our *selves* with our thinking selves. 'I think, therefore I am', René Descartes insisted; that at least he could be sure of. On the basis of this apparently unshakeable proposition, he set out to build up an entire system of reliable knowledge of the world, without recourse to prior authority. But this confidence in the undoubted *cogito*, the essential thinking self that I am, can also become a limitation on my knowledge of the world outside me. The proposition that Descartes so neatly crystallized has now become stout common sense: what I am, in essence, many people believe, is my consciousness, free to have personal opinions, make choices, follow its own logic. But paradoxically, that consciousness can also become a kind of prison, isolating me from any certainty about the world outside.

Within a generation or so of Descartes, John Locke would begin to register a distinct pessimism about whether the way the world appears in consciousness corresponds to the world as it actually is. We encounter objects through the experience of the senses, he believed, but how far can we trust our own sensations? In Locke's time the microscope and the telescope had both shown how much we miss when we look with the naked eye. What if our other senses are equally limited? Moreover, if consciousness is the place where we ourselves are to be found, all we can be sure of is the way sensations make themselves apparent to consciousness. The most we can count on, Locke complained, is the *idea* of the *sensation* of the object, which is a long way from certainty about the object itself, or about whether what we know corresponds to the way things are.

In other words, epistemology, or the study of what it is possible to know, is not the same as ontology, or the theory of what exists. Or is it? How can there be a theory of what exists, in the light of the limitations of consciousness? And if we have no certain knowledge of whatever exists, how can we be sure it exists at all?

If ontology is as shaky as that, what about epistemology itself? How can there be a study of what it is possible to know, when it begins to look as if it is not possible to know anything outside our own heads?

KANT v. HEGEL

Confronted by these arguments, which seem to go round in circles, Immanuel Kant, possibly the greatest of the Enlightenment philosophers, concluded that there must be a distinction between what we know and what exists. In Kant's view, we can know things only as they appear to us, within a framework of knowledge that we ourselves create. Beyond the appearances, there lies a realm of things-in-themselves, which is forever inaccessible to our knowledge.

In the next generation, however, Georg Wilhelm Friedrich Hegel refused to settle for this gloomy view of the limitations on human knowledge. With the boundless optimism of the early nineteenth century about what was possible, Hegel developed a system that would impose no limits on what we are able to know – on condition that the ultimate object of knowledge is consciousness itself.

Hegel's starting point is what he calls 'sense-certainty', our awareness at the level of the senses of the sheer existence of things in the world. Sense-certainty seems immediate, but in practice, Hegel makes clear, it depends on a separation between the knowing subject and the object of knowledge, or self and other. At the same time, human beings are driven, he believed, by a desire to do away with the opposition between subject and object, to abolish the *otherness* of the other. In consequence, *perception* supersedes sense-certainty as a way of containing this 'negation', or reconciling the antithesis that has emerged between the self and its objects of knowledge. Knowledge becomes a matter of perception.

Perception, however, is no more than my perception, or the perception available in my culture. Hegel was a historicist: he saw knowledge as culturally relative. What it is possible to know self-evidently varies from one historical moment to another. But he also believed that history had unfolded progressively until it reached the Enlightenment and the moment of Hegel's own work. For the first time, the Enlightenment offered the possibility of universal knowledge, more reliable than mere perception, where rational understanding opens up a world beyond the one we perceive, a supersensible world of things as they appear in (universal, rational) consciousness.

It is because he stopped at this point in the argument, Hegel insists, that Kant supposed the true being of things was unknowable. Hegel's next move is therefore crucial. He turns consciousness into its own object of knowledge. Enlightened, rational, universal consciousness is consciousness of the world as it is; the world is thus synonymous with consciousness of itself. In these circumstances there can be no failure of correspondence between consciousness and things-in-themselves. 'Reason is the certainty of consciousness that it is all reality. . . . The "I" which is an object for me is the sole object, is all reality and all that is present' (Hegel 1977: 140).

When rational consciousness fully knows itself, becomes its own other, uniting self and other without abolishing their difference, reason reaches the level of what Hegel calls *Geist*. The German word has no exact equivalent in English, but is variously translated as 'mind' or 'spirit'. 'Reason is Spirit', Hegel affirms, 'when its certainty of being all reality has been raised to truth, and it is conscious of itself as its own world, and of the world as itself' (1977: 263).

IDEALISM

Very few philosophers today would be willing to share Hegel's confidence in universal reason and the corresponding capacity of consciousness to contain – and thus constitute – the truth. Hegel called his own system absolute idealism, in the sense that it allotted primacy and authority to ideas and claimed that ideas could deliver the truth. As a philosophy, idealism sees ideas as the ultimate reality.

Hegel's incorporation of the world into consciousness might alternatively be understood to erase the world as anything more than an idea, and so to abolish the real. And even if few philosophers would subscribe to Hegel's system now, its influence is perceptible in the widespread idealism that links a number of influential cultural theorists, Judith Butler and Stanley Fish among them. What is the continuing appeal of a philosophical system that is extraordinarily difficult to interpret, and seems so exceptionally characteristic of its own time? Hegel's historical moment differed radically, after all, from ours, when the atrocities of two world wars and the repressions practised in the name of communism have significantly undermined the belief in progress. In the light of those events, what evidence is there that civilization is advancing in the direction of universal rational consciousness? So far, the twenty-first century has shown new divisions emerging between fundamentalisms grounded in apparently irreconcilable cultural differences, as the West confronts extremist Islamic violence not with diplomacy, nor even a serious effort to analyse its causes, but with bombs.

The appeal of idealism resides, I believe, in its completion of the Cartesian project. 'I think, therefore I am' slides easily into 'I think, and that is what matters'. 'I think' remains a proposition I can feel sure of, however much the world about me changes. Moreover, idealism affirms the sovereignty of the self. '"I am I", in the sense that the "I" which is an object for me is the sole object, is all reality and all that is present' (Hegel 1977: 140).

MIND–BODY DUALISM

Reassuring as idealism may be in an uncertain world, however, it depends on dividing the essence of human beings from their bodies and the world they inhabit. Descartes makes his certainty that he exists as a thinking being depend on a radical distinction between the *cogito* and everything else. He could conceive, he says, that he had no body, and that there was no world or place that he was in but, even so, he could not pretend that he was not thinking, doubting, conceiving. And so,

> From this I knew I was a substance whose whole essence or nature is solely to think, and which does not require any place or depend on any material thing in order to exist. Accordingly this 'I' – that is the soul by which I am what I am – is entirely distinct from the body.
>
> (Descartes 1988: 36)[1]

Of course, this distinction is conceptual. Descartes does not in the end deny the existence of the body and the world in which it finds itself. The argument will go through a number of stages, including the case for the existence of God, who would surely not set out to deceive us about such questions, in order to concede that the body exists, and that we are very closely joined to it, to the point where we form a single whole with it. What is more, there are probably other bodies like our own, and a material world to contain them. But these are issues on which we can be mistaken. Thinking alone remains certain; mind and materiality are different substances.

Much subsequent discussion in medicine and the social sciences would call in question the value of a conceptual distinction between mind and body. In our more secular world, psychiatry would probably give priority to the mind, but allow that its condition influences the body; sociobiology would be more likely to stress the continuity of human bodies with their animal ancestors, and see our thought processes as influenced by our evolutionary descent. Without attributing any final authority to any of these disciplines, it is easy to see by comparison how far Descartes's seventeenth-century philosophy takes for granted a supernatural Christian cosmos. Indeed, he insists that, even without a body, his soul 'would not fail to be whatever it is' (36). Not everyone in the twenty-first century would share this view. Sadly, for many of us, death puts an end to both *cogito* and body, as well as any supposed distinction of substance between them.

What Descartes subordinates, Hegel finally does away with, or at least subsumes. His system charts the ascent of the mind from sensuous awareness of the world to absolute knowledge, which is pure self-consciousness. The object changes as it becomes an object of knowledge. As consciousness adapts itself to objects, they in turn become components of consciousness (Hegel 1977: 54–5); the actual present world vanishes into the supersensible world of understanding (87–8); and at last, reason knows only essences, so that 'we can, strictly speaking, no longer talk of things at all' (143).

At the same time, the specificity of the individual self disappears too. In a move that goes way beyond Cartesian mind–body dualism, Hegel contains and erases personal consciousness within universal reason. Recognizing, like Descartes, that individual experience is prone to error, Hegel locates absolute knowledge in a universality that entails 'the externalization and vanishing of this particular "I"' (308).

LANGUAGE

How is this extraordinary feat accomplished? By way of language. Even if Hegel's system in its entirety no longer seems persuasive, his individual insights have proved extraordinarily influential. And his comments on language have repercussions for culturalism and post-structuralism alike.

Language in Hegel is the means of escape from the prison of individual consciousness and the source of confidence that universal knowledge is possible. Suppose we return to the apparent immediacy of sense-certainty. How can we record the experience, register the particularity of seeing a specific tree? With words like 'this' tree, 'here', 'now'. But these same words continue to apply elsewhere, when the moment has passed. When we have turned away from the tree towards the house opposite, and the sun has gone down, 'this' has become a house, 'here', where I am facing, 'now' in the dark. 'This', 'here', 'now' can apply to any number of objects (Hegel 1977: 59–65). It is the property of language to generalize. In an attempt to be as particular, as singular, as possible, Hegel says, I name 'this bit of paper', but language cannot reach the sensuous 'this', and since 'each and every bit of paper is "this bit of paper" . . . I have only uttered the universal all the time' (66).

Knowledge, then, deals in universals. It negates the particularity of sensation in favour of universality. What do we know about salt? That it is white, tart, granular . . . and these are general properties that differ from each other, while one or other of them may be shared with sugar or sand. Such knowledge is no longer single, personal, private, but shared, Hegel would say, universally.

Sadly, however, there is a price to pay for the community of enlightened minds that thus becomes available. Because language constrains what it is possible to say, we can no longer say what we mean. We set out to name the particular experience, but language insists on universalizing it.

> And since the universal is the true [content] of sense-certainty and language expresses this true [content] alone, it is just not possible for us ever to say, or express in words, a sensuous being that we *mean*.
>
> (Hegel 1977: 60)

Language allows no access to the uniqueness of things. Instead, it

> has the divine nature of directly reversing the meaning of what is said, of making it into something else, and thus not letting what is meant *get into words* at all.
>
> (66)

But there is worse to come. Language, which places things beyond reach, but which, as if in compensation, enables consciousness to know itself and to communicate with others, has the further effect of placing the self in its uniqueness equally beyond reach. Individuality has only 'an *imaginary* existence' (298). This unique self in its real existence is subsumed by a universal self that enters into a new kind of reality.

Paradoxically, it is language that permits the self to exist in its difference from others. But that very difference immediately disappears again in the generality that characterizes language:

in speech, self-consciousness, *qua independent separate individuality*, comes as such into existence, so that it exists *for others*. Otherwise the 'I', this *pure* 'I', is non-existent, is not *there*. . . . Language . . . contains it in its purity, it alone expresses the 'I', the 'I' itself. This *real* existence of the 'I' is, *qua* real existence, an objectivity which has in it the true nature of the 'I'. The 'I' is this particular 'I' – but equally the *universal* 'I'; its manifesting is also at once the externalization and vanishing of *this* particular 'I'.

(308)

There is no option. In Hegel's account, the silent, intuitive mind does not exist either as consciousness or in its separateness. Moreover, it cannot relate to others. 'The "I" that utters itself', he says, 'is *heard or perceived*'; but at the same time, 'That it is *perceived or heard* means that its *real existence dies away*' (309).

CULTURALISM

This paradox, whether derived direct from Hegel, or from Hegel filtered by others, and modified by subsequent developments, is the starting point, it seems to me, of cultural constructivism. Identity is culturally scripted; modes of reading are defined by interpretive communities; facts, like values, are social and political constructs; bodies materialize as the effect of speech acts. And it follows that, participating in culture as we do, we lose our individuality in a form of cultural determinism that has, in the end, no way of accounting for dissent, in the same way as it allows no independent place for the real.

   Such culturalist convictions reproduce Hegel's idealism with his insights. The world exists for us primarily as an idea; it exerts no significant determinations, except as '*a demand in and for language*, a "that which" which . . . calls to be explained, described, diagnosed' (Butler 1993: 67). Judith Butler explicitly echoes Hegel when she insists that the body is not 'an ontological-in-itself which only becomes available through a psyche'. 'That Kantian formulation', she goes on, 'requires to be reworked . . . in a more phenomenological register as an imaginary formation' (66). It is in the *Phenomenology of Spirit* that Hegel repudiates Kant's things-in-themselves, and identifies the real existence of the particular self as 'imaginary'.

Aware of all the twentieth century taught us about the irreducibility of cultural difference, culturalism rejects Hegel's Enlightenment conviction that absolute knowledge is possible as universal truth. It retains, however, his historicism, as well as his idealism, with the effect of erasing the real. Whatever resides outside culture is held to have no bearing on us: unnameable, it has no effects.

RESISTANCE

In consequence, culturalism allows only a very reduced place for resistance. A common critique of twentieth-century new historicism, for example, has emphasized its propensity to see all events as contributions to the survival of the existing social order. The homogeneous culture it defines allows no space for dissent (Belsey 1999: 15–18). Instead, minor revolts simply offer occasions for extending social control; crime legitimates an extension of the police.

This view is often attributed, erroneously, to Michel Foucault, whose own declared position was more complex. Resistance for Foucault is a necessary corollary of power: not its excuse and ally, but its defining alternative. If meaning depends on difference, power is imperceptible, unintelligible *as* power, where resistance is ruled out. That all social relations are also relations of power implies the possibility of struggle, not automatic submission (Foucault 1979: 95–6).

But how, if our social performance is culturally scripted, is resistance possible? In two ways. For one, social values contradict one another: a commitment to human rights, for instance, conflicts with homophobia. As the contest between them is played out in society, one side or the other comes to prevail. And for another, unconscious desire, formed in the place of the lost real, contradicts the instructions of the cultural script itself, pulls against it on behalf of other imperatives. These imperatives trace in the speaking being the contours of loss, and make themselves evident as dissatisfaction or restlessness.

PSYCHOANALYSIS

Psychoanalysis offers a quite different way to take account of Hegel's theory that language erases the real existence of the particular 'I'. Jacques Lacan considers this issue in 'The Signification of the Phallus', the essay that, rightly or wrongly, has so irritated feminists. Putting aside the problem of phallocentrism for the moment, we can see how Lacan takes up Hegel's story with a difference.

Language, Lacan proposes, subjects the world of things to its influence. In the Saussurean vocabulary he uses here,

> the signifier has an active function in determining certain effects in which the signifiable appears as submitting to its mark, by becoming through that passion the signified.
>
> (Lacan 1977: 284)

In other words, language reduces the world of things, in itself meaningless, but capable of signification ('the signifiable'), to meanings. In consequence, human beings become the 'material' of language, so that there 'resounds' or 'resonates' in them 'the relation of speech' (284). This means that they are able to be heard and perceived; the child who submits in this way to the meanings available can make demands, identify the needs all organisms experience, naming them hunger, thirst, or the effects of a stray safety pin in an uncomfortable place.

But, as in Hegel, there is a price to pay. In so far as the language always comes from outside, from the Other, as Lacan puts it, these demands return to us 'alienated' (286). Borrowing from an existing system of differences, dependent on other people's formulations, we cannot say exactly what we mean. Language generalizes. And to the degree that the child's request is generalized as the requirement to be loved, demand 'annuls (aufhebt) the particularity of everything that can be granted by transmuting it into a proof of love' (286).

So far, the vocabulary draws on Hegel, as well as Saussure, and the model might be seen as a specifically psychoanalytic appropriation of Hegel's account of the effects of language. But there follows a move which makes all the difference:

> It is necessary, then, that the particularity thus abolished should reappear *beyond* demand. . . . By a reversal that is not simply a negation of the negation, the power of pure loss emerges from the residue of an obliteration.
>
> (286–7)

What reappears beyond demand is not the lost needs, but unconscious desire. Obliteration of real, organic existence leaves its mark. Human beings are now to be seen as 'woven' (284), composites of the speaking beings they become and the real organisms they remain but can no longer reach.

The unconscious is not a fragment of the lost real, not simply a reversal of the first annulment, but a residue of obliteration itself, evident as a lack. While there is nothing missing in the real, there appears an absence at the level of the signifier, at the level, that is to say, of language and culture. This absence, the lack in what Lacan calls the symbolic order, marks the place of the repressed, no longer accessible to the speaking being, concealed from consciousness.

The lack is not one that can be met or filled. Desire is not in the end desire for *something* or *someone*, however much it names itself as love (and its corollary, hate). The succession of objects of desire that present themselves as able to satisfy it are no more, Lacan says, than stand-ins, substitutes at the level of demand, for an 'object' that is altogether less palpable. The task of the analyst is to make evident the unconscious desire that the analysand does not consciously intend or acknowledge.

Lacan's rejection of mind–body dualism is not a cheery 'wholism', therefore, in which mind and body are reconciled or reintegrated; nor is it a relaxed version, where they subsist alongside each other in perfect harmony. And it is emphatically not a return to nature and biologism, relocating the human essence in the body. Instead, the relationship between an organism and the driven human being it becomes, at the mercy of compulsions that seem to have no origin or explanation in rational consciousness, is precisely the enigma that psychoanalysis addresses.

His view is not, Lacan hastens to insist, a form of cultural constructivism:

> It should be made clear that this advocacy of man's relation to the signifier as such has nothing to do with a 'culturalist' position. . . . It is not a question of the relation between man and language as a social phenomenon.
>
> (284–5)

In other words, psychoanalysis concerns the inevitable loss that is the effect of a structural relationship between language and subjectivity, whatever the content of the language in question, and not simply a specific cultural or historical version of it. The unconscious desire that appears in the structural place of that loss is not, in this sense, culturally relative, even though the succession of objects of desire we can *name* as able to make us happy are culturally defined.

This is not to say, however, that psychoanalysis has no comment to make on our own historical moment. On the contrary. In particular, Lacan deplores the Cartesian dualism common sense seems to take for granted. He begins one of his earliest essays with the affirmation that psychoanalytic experience 'leads us to oppose any philosophy directly issuing from the *Cogito*' (1977: 1). Later, he names the transcendent consciousness as a source of *hubris* in contemporary culture:

> It is nonetheless true that the philosophical *cogito* is at the centre of the mirage that renders modern man so sure of being himself even in his uncertainties about himself, and even in the mistrust he has learned to practise against the traps of self-love.
>
> (165)

This mirage also constitutes the flip side of culturalism, the conviction that, as cultural subjects, we must be the collective origin of all aspects of our own condition. In the specific instance of sexual difference, Charles Shepherdson has perfectly encapsulated the self-indulgence of contemporary constructivism:

> sexual difference is not a human institution, and if in our theories we pretend that it is simply one more social construction, invented by a particular society (like democracy or Christianity), do we not

unwittingly sustain the humanistic (narcissistic) notion that 'man is the maker of all things'?

(Shepherdson 2000: 91)

'ANNA O.'

Just how sovereign is culture? To what extent do we obey the cultural script? There are many stories of resistance, but no one tells them better than Sigmund Freud, whose case histories emulate the detective stories he so enjoyed. The inaugural text of psychoanalysis, *Studies on Hysteria*, vividly recounts the problems of Elisabeth von R., who had pains in her thighs that seemed to have no organic cause, or Lucy R., the English governess, who at twenty-four had lost her sense of smell, but hallucinated an aroma of burnt pudding. From the point of view of the psychoanalytic challenge to mind–body dualism, however, as well as the possibility of resisting the cultural script, the most interesting of these early case histories is probably 'Anna O.' This is not Freud's at all, but the work of his co-author, Josef Breuer, though Freud would later annotate it, and clearly saw Anna's history as a milestone in the development of psychoanalysis.

In 1880 Anna developed a persistent cough, severe disturbances of vision, paralysis of the right arm and both legs, and partial paralysis of the neck muscles. These physiological symptoms could not be explained by conventional medicine, and appeared unaccountable in a young woman of twenty-one who had previously been perfectly healthy. Moreover, this condition was accompanied by alternating moods. In one she was unhappy and anxious, but otherwise relatively normal and characteristically sympathetic and kind; in the other she was, as she herself put it, 'naughty', displaying her 'bad self' (Freud and Breuer 1974: 76, 101). Her bad self was abusive, and threw cushions at people, ripping the buttons off her bedclothes. After these episodes, which she named 'absences', she remembered nothing about them, though she might comment on the gaps in her train of conscious thought (76). In addition, she became unable to speak German, her native language. Breuer tried what the fledgling science of the 'unconscious' could do where the doctors had failed. (It was Breuer who first used the term, and in this text (100).)

The worst of her symptoms, he discovered, could be traced to a night in July. The father she loved was seriously ill, and while her mother was away, Anna was left alone to nurse him. Sitting by his bedside, she fell into a 'waking dream', and seemed to see a snake coming from the wall to bite her father. Apparently, there may have been snakes in the field behind the house in the country, where the family was staying, and this might have motivated the image. She tried to keep off the hallucinatory snake, but 'it was as though she was paralysed'. At the same time, 'language failed her: she could find no tongue in which to speak', until eventually she remembered some nursery rhymes in English, and then she found herself able to communicate – and pray – in that language (92–3).

What was the meaning of Anna O.'s encounter with the uncanny snake, and the severe disorder, at once physiological and psychological, it brought about? Breuer does not say, though he insists (optimistically, as subsequent investigations have revealed (Borch-Jacobsen 1999)), that as soon as she had reproduced her waking dream for him under hypnosis, her condition improved dramatically. With hindsight, however, and in the light of more than a century of subsequent psychoanalytic theory, it is not hard to develop on the basis of Breuer's text a (possible, partial) reading of Anna O.'s waking dream.

Anna 'was markedly intelligent', Breuer tells us, 'with an astonishingly quick grasp of things and penetrating intuition. She possessed a powerful intellect which would have been capable of digesting solid mental pabulum and which stood in need of it – though without receiving it after she had left school' (Freud and Breuer 1974: 73). It was Anna O. who invented the phrase, the 'talking cure', to describe Breuer's treatment of her symptoms (83). She was fluent in several European languages. However, according to the case history, 'This girl, who was bubbling over with intellectual vitality, led an extremely monotonous existence in her puritanically-minded family' (74).

In July the father she adored fell ill, and for the first few months Anna devoted all her energy to nursing him, until in December her own health broke down, and she was no longer able to care for him. She developed a cough, which began at her father's bedside when she heard dance music next door, felt a sudden longing to be there, and then was overcome with self-reproach. After the waking dream of the snake, the cough was compounded by the more severe symptoms. And she could no longer speak her own language.

When she is well, we might construe, Anna reproduces the cultural script, and duly performs the proper meaning of the word 'woman' in Vienna in 1880. She stays at home, where her intelligence has no outlet; but she puts others first and nurses her sick father, when she would rather go dancing. In her illness she rejects this meaning in its entirety, and the language in which it takes its place, refusing the obligations of 'womanhood'. All she can remember are nursery rhymes in a foreign language, the culturally transmitted but alien inscription of childhood and its irresponsibility. The hallucination surely fulfils a desire that cannot be consciously acknowledged, in which she neglects her responsibilities as a nurse by day-dreaming. And in this state, she makes no effort to save her father's endangered life.

The snake may have its origin in the field behind the house, but might it not also be derived from the biblical story of the Garden of Eden, a cultural memory textually inscribed? And what it promises is another, forbidden identity outside the authorized meaning of woman: rebellious, irresponsible, and perhaps knowing. In her waking dream Anna glimpses an escape from her linguistically defined destiny. No wonder her first response to the recognition of this thrilling, terrifying, wicked possibility is an impulse to pray, and no wonder that she has to punish herself for resisting the cultural script by becoming ill. Her illness, it is worth adding, secures for this intellectually starved woman the practically undivided attention of an exceptionally intelligent, young male doctor.

Where does her resistance come from? Not from consciousness, evidently: Anna loves her father and doesn't consciously want to be rid of him. But not from 'nature', either. And still less from the body. The unconscious represents the residue of the obliteration performed by language of the instinctual, organic self. In Lacan's terms, Anna's forbidden impulse to go dancing, and her even more inadmissible wish not to have to nurse her father day and night, demonstrate the reappearance beyond the symbolic order, beyond anything she can recognize or control, of a desire that stems from pure loss. Dancing and day-dreaming are not an end in themselves, not the final object of unconscious desire, but stand-ins for something that would take the place of the missing real. Unconscious desire marks its loss to the speaking subject.

When smokers contracted lung cancer without knowing what caused it, they encountered the real. If medieval sailors nudged at the edge of the world, but failed to fall off, they encountered the resistance of the real. This is the real that exists outside us as a limitation on our power to make the world in our own image of it. In the psychic life of speaking beings, meanwhile, the real of the organisms they also are is lost to consciousness. This particularity is cancelled by the Other of language. But what is lost reappears as a residue, unconscious desire for something else, which may, as in this case, be deadly in its aim.

Anna's forgotten, repressed, waking dream is subsequently 'written' on her body as a symptom, in the form of the paralysis which follows. Release from her illness is possible only when she remembers the event under hypnosis and narrates it in words to Breuer, 'rewrites' it at the level of the signifier. Inscribed on Anna's body, presented, however inadequately, in the talking cure, and re-presented, however partially, in Breuer's case history, the hallucination of the snake reveals another identity for Anna O., another subject position, or perhaps more than one, in excess of the identification her culture offers as the proper, self-sacrificing meaning of what it is to be a woman.

What she resists is the specific cultural script available to respectable young women, especially in Orthodox Jewish families, in late nineteenth-century Vienna. But the possibility of resistance is structural, a dissatisfaction characteristic of the uneasy conjunction between a human organism and the Otherness of language which erases the particularity of real needs. Anna went on resisting the destiny her culture prescribed for her, but in due course she found a culturally permissible outlet for it in feminism. The non-fictional Anna O., Bertha Pappenheim, went on to give much of her subsequent energy to the emerging cause of women's emancipation (Jones 1953: 248). She translated Mary Wollstonecraft's *A Vindication of the Rights of Women* into the German she had now recovered, and wrote a play about sexual exploitation called *A Woman's Right* (Appignanesi and Forrester 1992: 78). She never married.

THE ALTERNATIVE TO IDEALISM

Psychoanalysis, then, repudiates idealism and the mind–body dualism it entails, but without returning to the bluff empiricism that sees the materiality of things as 'obvious'. Freud insisted throughout his work on the organic life of his patients, but he also insisted that the symptoms which so commonly marked their bodies did not originate there. The drive, he affirmed, was the representative in the psyche of an instinct, and thus to be found 'on the frontier between the mental and the physical' (Freud 1977a: 83).[2] That instinct itself no longer exists as such in the speaking being, but its residue survives in the psyche to exert an influence on mind and body, or mind-and-body, since in this account the two interact in a way that renders them no longer so easily distinguishable.

In consequence, the cultural script is never absolute. It plays a crucial role, of course: we cannot account for Anna O.'s behaviour without reference to the specificity of her cultural moment. At the same time, that cultural moment does not fully explain the 'absences' that made her unaware of her surroundings, the 'bad self' that threw cushions at her visitors and tore the buttons off her bedclothes, or the loss of her own culture in its inscription in her native language. For that we need to recognize what culture withholds, or the inability of the script to cover the lack that appears in culture itself.

The abolished particularity returns as resistance, marking the speaking being's loss of the unnameable real, which is still there, but no longer there-for-a-subject. This resistance makes itself felt not only in individual experience, but also as incoherences in the apparent homogeneity of culture itself. A cultural criticism that takes this into account is able to acknowledge the silences that mark the inscriptions of culture, the complexity and the hesitations of the texts, as well as their noisier affirmations.

3

THE LACANIAN REAL

THE PARADOX OF PSYCHOANALYSIS

What gives psychoanalysis a special purchase on culture in general, and the traditional Western opposition between mind and body, or ideas and matter, in particular?

Psychoanalysis develops as paradox. At the very moment when the distinction between the arts and sciences was in the process of sedimentation, confirming the existence of a single and determining antithesis between culture and the material world, psychoanalysis emerged across the line between them. In the early twentieth century, only science had serious intellectual credibility, and Freud claimed scientific status for his fledgling discipline accordingly. Anna O.'s symptoms are identified as paraphasia, paresis, a *tussis nervosa* and diplopia (though the text carefully, but apparently casually, explains in lay terms just what all this means). And yet this medical vocabulary takes its place in a highly readable case history that begins in enigma and ends with closure, like any good classic realist narrative of the period.

Science is crucially experimental: if its hypotheses can't in principle be tested and falsified, it isn't science. Psychoanalysis offered hypthotheses, and generalized its empirical findings; it was certainly not an art in the way that writing a poem is an art; but Anna's case could hardly be re-enacted in the laboratory. Moreover, Freud traced the central concept of the new science, the Oedipus complex, to a work of fiction, a play by Sophocles. And he offered a talking cure for physiological symptoms.

Despite its founder's best efforts, psychoanalysis refused to reproduce the widening gap between the arts and sciences. How could it? Its main preoccupation in the early days was sex, where people meet as bodies, but where, even so, the success of the encounter owes a good deal to the terms on which they meet. It is hard to imagine willing human sex without fantasy. What does it for you? Romantic love is a non-negotiable condition for many – supported by a whole industry of flowers, Valentine cards and candle-lit dinners. For others it might be power, or the surrender of power, or being treated as a baby, or punished like a naughty boy. No wonder psychoanalysis could not settle for a dualism of mind and body.

Instead, it turns on the paradox of the speaking being:

> There is, according to analytic discourse, an animal that happens to be endowed with the ability to speak [finds itself speaking, 1975: 81] and who, because he inhabits the signifier, is thus a subject of it. Henceforth, everything is played out for him at the level of fantasy, but at the level of a fantasy that can be perfectly disarticulated in a way that accounts for the following – that he knows a lot more about things than he thinks when he acts.
>
> (Lacan 1998: 88)

This quotation from Lacan's twentieth seminar, conducted in 1972–3, expands a view he had formulated in similar terms fifteen years earlier, that unconscious desire belongs to 'an animal at the mercy of language' (1977: 264). The quotation from *Seminar 20* points to three distinct levels of human existence: first, the animal, the human organism in the real; second, the world of fantasy, of conscious social and cultural reality, that language invites us to inhabit; and third, the un-conscious, the element subtracted from consciousness that knows, none the less, more than we think, or more than our conscious thinking makes explicit. These three levels interact with each other at every moment of human existence – until death. And death presents yet another paradox.

DEATH

The subject is what speaks. Language makes us subjects, but in the process permits us to know that we shall rejoin the real in the end. We shall die. Because meaning depends on difference, the verb 'to be' brings with it the capacity not to be. As Lacan puts it, 'It is in the signifier and insofar as the subject articulates a signifying chain that he comes up against the fact that he may disappear from the chain of what he is' (1992: 295).

But the relation between language and death goes deeper. The subject's own constitution in language brings about the 'death' of the real for the subject. In that sense, the possibility of absence from the signifying chain is there at the inaugural moment of the speaking being. The absent real anticipates a future absence for the subject itself, marks subjectivity as finite, temporary.

Lacan borrows from Heidegger the awareness of our own death as a perpetual condition of human beings which, whether we know it or not, shapes and influences everything we do. (If you doubt it, imagine a world that had conquered death, or in which death was impossible. How much would be different? Sex, partnerships, parent-hood, work, adventures . . . . If our lives were not finite, would anything remain the same?) In that sense,

> when we wish to attain in the subject what was before the serial articulations of speech, and what is primordial to the birth of symbols, we find it in death, from which his existence takes on all the meaning it has.
>
> (Lacan 1977: 105)

The knowledge of our own mortality is characteristically human. So too is the commemoration of the dead. All known societies have burial practices and funeral rites. It is from tombs, to varying degrees grand, imposing, or pathetic, that we derive much of our knowledge of vanished cultures.

Moreover, many societies have made their tombs exceptionally visible, as if to remind the living of their own finitude. Prehistoric burial mounds drew attention to themselves by standing out above the surrounding landscape. Medieval churches came to enclose ever more spectacular monumental structures, which increasingly mimicked the churches themselves in their flamboyant adornment. The Egyptians placed the pyramids beyond the green line that marked the limit of the flood plain of the Nile, in a desert where no life was possible, but they made sure that this necropolis was visible from the living city. Death, then, puts itself on show. Or rather, monuments to the dead do so. They symbolize a loss. Pyramids, massive, substantial, material, contain, in the mummified corpses they house, no more than the trace of the once living, moving, powerful beings they memorialize.

In all this display of grandeur, however, death itself remains oddly unpresentable. The experience, the way it *feels*, retains its mystery, since those who have known it are by definition no longer here to tell us about it. Our own death is difficult to imagine. Freud pointed out that it is virtually impossible to do so, and when we try, we find that we ourselves are present in the imagined scene, hovering somewhere close by (1985a: 77). We cannot represent death to ourselves, even though we can name it, and see it staged in any number of genres from classical tragedy to Hollywood movies. As Roland Barthes might have said, 'Every night on TV, someone dies'. But this is someone else's death: our own remains oddly elusive, imaginatively hard to conceive.

Death thus constitutes a paradoxically absent presence in the symbolic order, and in that respect it not only exemplifies the real as unknowable, but typifies at the same time the lost object of immediate experience, subsumed, supplanted, and yet not finally abolished by the signifier.

Why is this? Because, Lacan would say, while there is nothing lacking in the real, there is always something missing in the symbolic, but this is an absence that makes its presence felt. As Saussure proposed, language is a system of differences 'without positive terms' (Saussure 1974: 120). In other words, nothing in the world anchors the meanings that language itself produces. Language, in consequence, *is not to be trusted*. The signifier seems to evoke the existence of something on the other side of it, but refuses to tell us what this is. Ordinary language, for example, locates an intention, a reason or a truth 'behind' what is said. But there is no access to this place 'behind' the words; whatever inhabits it remains undefined, conjectural. The signifier, then, appears as a veil, but one that veils the unknown, perhaps nothing, a possible absence, the potential absence, even, of the subject itself.

In his seminar on the gaze, Lacan invokes the classical story of the competition between Zeuxis and Parrhasios to see which of them could paint a more realistic picture. Zeuxis thought he had won the contest when he portrayed grapes so lifelike that birds came and pecked at them. But he was wrong. His rival painted a veil so convincing that Zeuxis asked him to show what he had depicted behind it (Lacan 1979: 103).

Whether as an image or words, scientific equation or logical notation, the signifier veils whatever might be there. A symbol, whether story, picture or monument, constitutes evidence only, Lacan says, 'of the latency with which any signifiable is struck, when it is raised (*aufgehoben*) to the function of signifier' (1977: 288). In Lacan's account, it is this latency, not truth, nor any kind of certainty beyond the conviction that we are able not to be, that gives our existence what meaning it has – including our sexual existence.

A STRANGE SEDUCTION

'To His Coy Mistress', which brings sex and death together, must present one of the most curious invitations in the world. 'Give me your virginity', it says in effect, 'or give it to worms'. That worms devour corpses is widely acknowledged, even if it remains an unlikely thought in a love poem. That worms might wriggle their way into the vagina, however, offers a distinctively repulsive version of this familiar truth. At the same time, the poem evidently does not repel readers: Andrew Marvell's text is among the most widely anthologized of all love poems in English.

Divided into three main sections, three 'paragraphs', the poem devotes its first twenty lines to a prolonged courtship that develops across great distances and by almost imperceptible stages: the lover promises a hundred years to praise the woman's eyes and forehead; two hundred for each breast; and thirty thousand for the rest of her body. In these immensities of time and space the couple would barely move: 'We would sit down, and think which way/To walk, and pass our long love's day.' This 'vegetable love' would take up the whole of human history, growing to huge proportions, but slowly – because that is what she deserves.

Yet prefacing this ideal picture (just *how* ideal is it, in practice?), a conditional verb identifies it as impossible: 'Had we but world enough, and time . . . .' They don't. What faces them is not a glorious and protracted romance, but instead, at line 23 of a 46-line poem, a great emptiness: 'yonder all before us lie/Deserts of vast eternity'. In the exact centre of this sophisticated display of signifying practice, the name of a silence. The middle section of the poem dwells on the power of death to destroy all that the first part has so slowly and painstakingly assembled: her beauty, his praise, her aloofness, their ultimate embrace. If the 'marble vault' designed to enclose her is cold and lifeless, the worms, paradoxically, live all the more vigorously as they turn her 'quaint honour' to dust. And so with what looks like perfect logic, the poem concludes, 'Now, therefore . . . let us sport us while we may'.

Instead of languishing in time's slow-moving jaws, the text urges, they should act at once, 'like amorous birds of prey'. There is very little romance in this image, and still less in the proposition that follows, which is neither ideal nor lyrical, though perhaps the sexual fantasy is the more intense for that:

Let us roll all our strength, and all
Our sweetness, up into one ball:
And tear our pleasures with rough strife,
Thorough the iron gates of life.

Sex, the opposite of death, becomes its double in a struggle that aligns the lovers with falcons, as they devour their pleasures. Recognizing their subjection to mortality, they will in consequence take charge of their own fate, and go to meet the death they have no choice but to confront in due course. The awareness of their eventual absence from the signifying chain alters the meaning of sex, moves it out of the realm of romantic and uneventful contemplation towards urgent action.

If this were an actual situation, we might well accuse the speaker of a shameful opportunism and stop at that. But the poem we have, whatever its origins in Marvell's biography, if any, survives as pure text, and it is hard to believe that the admiration it evidently continues to elicit is purely for its forceful chat-up line. Not only does it bring into explicit proximity the most pressing topics of all good fiction, desire and mortality. In addition, it demonstrates, not just in its logic, but also in the shocking image of the penetrating worms, the imbrication of the one in the meaning of the other.

THE DRIVE AND THE *OBJET A*

Sex and death are also the most pressing topics of psychoanalysis, and Lacan was to develop an account of their relationship on the basis of Freud's later work. Specifically, if death intensifies desire, desire in turn can always evoke mortality, just as it does in Marvell's poem:

> the coming into play of the signifier in the life of man enables him to bring out the meaning of sex. Namely, that for man, because he knows the signifiers, sex and its significations are always capable of making present the presence of death.
>
> (Lacan 1979: 257)

This assertion takes its place in a discussion of what Lacan calls 'the *objet a*':

> It is a question of this privileged object, discovered by analysis, of that object whose very reality is purely topological, of that object around which the drive moves . . . the *objet a*.
>   This object supports that which, in the drive, is defined and specified by the fact that the coming into play of the signifier in the life of man enables him to bring out the meaning of sex.
>
> (1979: 257)

What is this privileged, but purely topological, object that links sex and death, an object that analysis discovers and around which the drive moves?

Zeuxis wanted to look behind the veil of the paint that constituted his rival's picture. The psychoanalytic subject longs to look behind the veil of the signifier, but what it seeks there is not so much the forgotten, repressed real, not that part of itself, or its continuity with the world, cut off by the symbolic and lost. Instead, it looks for the object and cause of its own desire, an identifiable something that would fill the gap created by the loss of the real. This object that motivates and perpetuates desire took on increasing importance for Lacan. In *Seminar 7* in 1959–60, he named it the Thing (*das Ding*); later, the Thing disappeared, to be remodelled as the *objet a*.

We need to go back a bit. For much of his life Freud insisted that the unconscious motor force of all human life was sexual. But during and after the First World War, his work begins to demonstrate a mounting conviction that there must be another drive that presses towards death. How else to account for the sustained carnage of that extraordinary and unheralded episode of history? *Beyond the Pleasure Principle*, published in 1920, begins by proposing an antithesis between the life-affirming sexual drive towards pleasure and, in contrast, the death drive that seeks inertia for the organism, but may equally be projected outwards by the subject as aggression against others.

As Freud's argument here unfolds, however, the two principles refuse to stay apart. On the one hand, there often seems to be an element of aggression in the sexual act; on the other, the pleasure principle too seeks release from tension, and so shares the aim of the death drive. Do they, then, support rather than oppose each other? Jacques Derrida has brilliantly deconstructed the opposition between the two (1987a), in this instance ably supported by Freud himself, who concluded his book with disarming honesty by admitting that he was not satisfied with a theory that remained purely speculative. He was left, he confessed, with

> a host of other questions to which we can at present find no answer. We must be patient and await fresh methods and occasions of research. We must be ready, too, to abandon a path that we have followed for a time, if it seems to be leading to no good end.
>
> (Freud 1984: 338)

(Sadly, all too few people are generally ready to follow his example!)

Beginning where Freud had left off, but going back to take account of a passage from 'Instincts and their Vicissitudes', published five years earlier (Freud 1984: 136–8), Lacan condensed the two drives into one. His rereading of Freud acknowledges only one drive, and it is both life-giving and deadly. *Seminar* 7 attends primarily to the quest for pleasure, which Lacan locates on the side of the signifier. Love is allied with pleasure, a form of sublimation, separable from desire itself.

But Lacan also brings pleasure together with death here in his account of tragedy. Where Freud roots his theory in the story of Oedipus, Lacan (as a child of Freud?), defies his phallocentric reputation and takes as his heroic protagonist Antigone, daughter of Oedipus and offspring, therefore, of an incestuous marriage. On the basis of the organic bond with her brother, Antigone is impelled to bury him against Creon's law, and to confront death as the inevitable punishment for her deed. Lacan sees Antigone as heroic because, like Marvell's lovers, she assumes her fate, her *Até*, 'atrocious' though it is. For Lacan, she represents human sovereignty in the face of death:

> Antigone appears as *autonomos*, as a pure and simple relationship of the human being to that of which he miraculously happens to be the bearer, namely, the signifying cut that confers on him the indomitable power of being what he is in the face of everything that may oppose him.
>
> (1992: 282)

Rather than languish as the victims of incompleteness that the signifier makes us, we are enabled by the same signifier to desire not to remain at its mercy. We can, in other words, want not to be. Marvell's lovers, who cannot make the sun stand still, will make him run, the poem defiantly affirms. Antigone, in Lacan's account, just as defiantly precipitates her own death. It is because she loves her brother that she 'pushes to the limit the realization of something that might be called the pure and simple desire of death as such. She incarnates that desire' (1992: 282).

Lacan's death drive bears very little resemblance to Freud's, which depends on the thesis that the organism prefers stasis, or inertia. We do not seek annihilation, Lacan says, for the sake of restoring equilibrium. But he does draw on Freud's proposal that the organism is driven to die at its own time and in its own way (Freud 1984: 311–12). In Lacan the death drive operates in the speaking being, at the level of the signifier, and seeks what he calls 'the second death'. This is not just physical extinction (the first death), which might take place at any time, by accident. Instead, the second death entails the full recognition of what we are, which is to say, of course, what we are *not*: not complete, not knowing, not immortal. The tragic hero acts on this understanding, assumes the destiny of a being-for-death and, when the time comes, willingly accedes to the state of non-being that is the outcome of the human condition.

At this stage of Lacan's work the object of the drive is identified as the Thing. An archaic, maternal, forbidden and impossible object of desire, the Thing is 'both living and dead' (1992: 300), at once life-giving and deadly. Lacan's name for it is partly ironic, since no such object exists in the real; at the same time, there is the suggestion of a pun in French on *la Chose* and the *cause* of desire that we attribute to the Thing. The Thing is 'that which in the real, the primordial real, I will say, suffers from the signifier' and 'presents itself' to the analyst in the gap produced by the signifying cut (1992: 118). Constructed retroactively to occupy the space of pure loss that is left by the erasure of the real, the Thing marks the place where the real was, constitutes itself as filling the emptiness that resides there for the speaking being.

Subsequently the object of the drive is renamed by the even more evasive term, *objet a*, and located more firmly at the level of demand. Lacan also calls it the *petit a*, to differentiate the little 'a' from the *Autre*, the big Other, which is language itself. Little Ernst's wooden reel offers an example of the *objet a*. In *Beyond the Pleasure Principle* Freud recounts the story of his grandson, who was greatly attached to his mother. At the age of one and a half, the child invented a game which he played again and again. This involved throwing away a wooden reel attached to a piece of string with a sound his grandfather, perhaps optimistically, interpreted as 'fort' ('gone'), and then recovering it with a joyful '*da*' ('there'). Freud reads this game as a way for Ernst to allow his mother to go away without protesting:

for the child the reel compensated for her absences, took her place (Freud 1984: 283–6).

It was the first action, throwing away the reel, that the child repeated tirelessly. This construction of a symbolic opposition between two terms, '*fort/da*', with the emphasis on the first, marks, Lacan affirms, the advent of language, of the signifying subject, and the splitting off of the real that that entails. What Ernst translates into representation, as he throws the symbolic reel, is not a need that might require his mother's return. On the contrary, he does not even look at the door in expectation of her return. Nor in Lacan's reading does the reel symbolize the child's mother as such. Instead, the object attached to the string represents a part of himself, *stands in for* the child's loss of continuity with the world around him, replaces and supplants the lost real of the connection that meets his needs, the particularity of his organic *relationship* with his mother. The reel takes the place of the real in the symbolic. And Lacan adds his own story to Freud's. He too, he says, has seen a child traumatized by the fact that he was going away, and has returned to find the same child ready to fall asleep on the shoulder of 'the living signifier that I had become' (1979: 62–3).

The wooden reel, this 'privileged object', that has emerged from the primal separation between the subject and the organism, from the 'self-mutilation' that cuts off the possibility of encountering the real, is the *objet a* (1979: 83), and it is in itself nothing much. Indeed, by way of compensation, it is nothing at all. Ernst will go on to abandon the plaything, but not the lack it symbolizes. And in later life he will no doubt seek a succession of stand-ins to fill this lack. None of them, however, will fully do so. Like the wooden reel, the object of love can never replace what is lost. Instead, 'that's not it'. '"That's not it" means that, in the desire of every demand, there is but the request for object *a*, for the object that would satisfy jouissance' (1998: 126).

No such object exists. As 'the void presupposed by a demand', the *objet a* represents non-being more explicitly than the Thing (1998: 126). It constitutes the nothing that is to be found behind the veil, the object-cause, both object and cause, of desire. In love, 'I love in you something more than you – the *objet petit a*' (1979: 263). Like the Thing, it has no existence in the real, since no actual object can satisfy the unconscious desire that pure loss serves to perpetuate.

THE REAL

The *objet a*, then, is not the real. Instead, it exists at the level of demand, as whatever would – if it could – fill the gap created by the fact that the real is lost to the subject. Meanwhile, the real itself remains in Lacan's account . . . well, real. During his first Seminar in 1954, he described the relation between the real and the symbolic in perfectly Saussurean terms:

> One can only think of language as a network, a net over the entirety of things, over the totality of the real. It inscribes on the plane of the real this other plane, which we here call the plane of the symbolic.
>
> (1988a: 262)

As he says here, signification and the real exist at different levels. In consequence, the signifier neither meets nor matches a referent, but differentiates a world that is capable of being invested with signification. Nearly two decades later, in *Seminar 20*, he would reformulate the point. Meaning-effects evoke the assumption that they must be caused by the referent, but this is not so: the two are not aligned, not adjusted to one another (1975: 23). In each case, the symbolic order misses the real. The following year he would affirm, 'The real is what does not depend on my idea of it' (Fink 1995: 142).

There are conceptual developments in between, as we might expect: in *Seminar 11*, for example, the real can be the place of events so traumatic that it must never be confronted, even in dreams. Psychoanalysis is thus called to undertake an encounter that is always missed 'with a real that eludes us' (1979: 53). It is only to the degree that psychoanalysis is able to register the impossibility of touching it that 'a certain real may be reached' (1998: 22).

The more improbable interpretations of Lacan appeal for support to work that is not yet available. As far as this is concerned, I reluctantly concede, with Derrida, that 'For the moment, I shall have to leave in suspense the question of whether, in later texts or in the seminars (published or unpublished, accessible or inaccessible)' Lacan contradicted himself (Derrida 2003: 134). But broadly, the real remains in place as what exists, but ex-sists the speaking being, is left outside the subject.

Even if the real is not there-for-a-subject, knowledge is capable of making inroads into it. This includes scientific knowledge, as well, of course, as the knowledge Freud inaugurated. The concept of the drive, for example, expanded our understanding to the degree that it mapped what had previously been unknown, because 'it traced its way in the real that it set out to penetrate' (Lacan 1979: 163). And Lacan compares psychoanalysis with the work of 'a Newton, an Einstein, a Planck', 'in the sense that all these fields are characterized by tracing in the real a new furrow in relation to the knowledge that might from all eternity be attributed to God' (1979: 127). God, if he existed, would have direct access to the real, of course, and would, indeed, be part of it. Lacan's world has very little place, however, for the supernatural.

He was drawn to mathematics, on the other hand, as a signifying system that does not delude us into supposing that it provides an account of the real. Mathematics is self-contained, a system of symbols that does not claim to represent the world. And yet, it too has its hour. In 1973, in a television interview designed to make psychoanalysis easy (not all that easy, you might conclude: he calls 'reality' 'a grimace of the real' (1990: 6)), Lacan was asked what it is possible to know. Nothing, he answers, that does not have the structure of a language. Even so, mathematics, 'using no apparatus other than a form of language', 'was able to bring about the moon landing, where thought becomes witness to a performance of the real' (1990: 36) or, in the original French, 'which testifies to an irruption of a real for thought' (1973b: 59).

The real, then, surrounds us. It also inhabits us as the condition of our ex-sistence. Human beings remain uneasy composites, the conjunction of an unreachable real organism and the subjects they become. The unconscious is not the real, nor the repository of the real, but the consequence of its loss. Driven though it is, and constituted by culturally constructed images of reality, the subject remains ultimately empty. A drive is not an instinct, but its representative in the psyche, like a delegate sent to take its place. Lacan insists that the drive is not to be understood as the pressure of a need, such as hunger or thirst. Nor is it the incursion into the mind of the real, living organism (1979: 164). But the real of the organism *as lost to the subject* remains the condition of the existence of the drive. 'The real . . . is the mystery of the speaking body, the mystery of the unconscious' (1998: 131).

4

ŽIŽEK AGAINST LACAN

SLAVOJ ŽIŽEK

In my account of the Lacanian real, I have stressed the distinction between the Thing and the *objet a* on the one hand, and the real on the other, because Slavoj Žižek tends in the name of Lacan to conflate them, to identify the real with the void, and thus to recuperate Lacan for idealism. Žižek's dazzling cultural criticism is now more widely read than Lacan's more esoteric texts, and is often mistaken for the guide to Lacanian theory it so wittily promises (1991, 1992a, 1992b). In my view, however, Žižek obscures one of the differentiating, and thus defining, aspects of psychoanalysis in an increasingly idealist world.

What, then, is Žižek's project and, more generally, why is idealism a problem? In this chapter I shall propose that there are good reasons why we should reaffirm Lacan's own non-idealist version of psychoanalysis as an alternative.

Žižek himself announces his own programme as designed 'to reassert the Cartesian subject' (1999a: 2) by means of a 'Lacanian reading of the problematic of subjectivity in German Idealism' (10). His own preface to *The Žižek Reader* declares this commitment in more unequivocal terms:

My work relies on the full acceptance of the notion of modern subjectivity elaborated by the great German Idealists from Kant to Hegel: for me, this tradition forms the unsurpassable horizon of our philosophical experience, and the core of my entire work is the endeavour to use Lacan as a privileged intellectual tool to reactualize German Idealism.

(1999b: ix)

Žižek's manner is characteristically mischievous, impertinent, outrageous. Exuberant, vehement, unexpected and profound by turns, his writing challenges all the rules of academic composition. How seriously, then, should we take this *enfant terrible* of high theory and low jokes when he defines his own project as the reaffirmation of idealism? My answer is, perfectly seriously.

I should say at once that Žižek is brilliant: prolific, provocative, a thinker to be reckoned with in the world that needs such writers. I differ from him, however, in finding his work more original, more inventive, and less Lacanian, than he claims – and I do not share his commitment to idealism.

Žižek follows Lacan in locating at the heart of the subject the single drive that links sex and death, and he owes to the later Lacan of *Seminar 7* onwards the intense emphasis on the involvement of the death drive in desire. The gap between the real and the symbolic is, Žižek reaffirms, irreducible, but for him a repressed residue of the unsymbolizable real forms a 'traumatic kernel' at the heart of the human being which resists assimilation into consciousness. Like Hegel's world of sense-certainty, Žižek's real is subsumed by the subject, and he brings Hegel together with Lacan to find this moment marked by irreparable trauma. The damage to the signifying subject is projected outwards as an antagonism that all social programmes need to take into account. Liberal democracy tries in vain to civilize it, totalitarianism to obliterate it. The implication of Žižek's work is that we should try to think beyond either if we are to find a way of reducing the destructiveness of human beings towards each other.

He goes further than Lacan, however, in divorcing the real from the organic. *The Sublime Object of Ideology*, the book that made Žižek famous in the West in 1989, clearly locates the real as Žižek understands it.

For him the real constitutes a structured absence, the void, finally empty. In Lacan, by contrast, the real is represented as emptiness *at the level of the signifier*, but it is not denied; indeed, there is nothing missing in the real itself. Žižek insists that the real is, in the end, *no more than* the inability to find its own inscription, '*nothing but this impossibility*' (1989: 173). The real is necessary to set the story of the subject in motion, Žižek says; it must be presupposed, to the extent that it is observable in its effects; but it remains an *absent* cause; it does not exist 'somewhere beyond the symbolic order' (173) in any non-signified positivity as substance (162–3). On the contrary, 'in itself it is nothing at all, just a void, an emptiness in a symbolic structure marking some central impossibility' (173), a position that cannot, by definition, be occupied (156). As 'the rock upon which every attempt at symbolization stumbles', the real dissolves, none the less, when we try to grasp it (169).

The 'Real' itself (Žižek consistently names it with a capital letter, investing it with portent and mystery) is thus the absent object-cause of desire, and is consequently synonymous with the *objet a*, a Hitchcockian MacGuffin that does not exist but exerts determinations in the psyche, none the less (163). The traumatic kernel of the real that survives in the unconscious resists assimilation into the symbolic order, and interrupts the smooth flow of the signifying exchange (1992a: 23). But, like the Thing, it is in itself no more than a construct. Since he conflates the real with the Thing, Žižek insists that the real is produced retroactively as a purely psychical phenomenon. Delighting in paradox, he asserts that the 'Real Thing is a fantasmatic spectre' (2002: 32). The traumatic moment of its constitution represents the advent of the death drive, to be projected outwards as social antagonism. This hostility is directed towards hate-figures, the sublime objects of ideology, invented to screen the unbearable absence of the real and the impossibility of *jouissance*. (I shall have more to say about these sublime objects in Chapter 9.)

In a breath-taking essay on Hegel's account of 'the night of the world', Žižek rounds up Kant and Hegel against Heidegger, to argue that the real as 'pure, not-yet-fashioned "multitude"', a totality of things, always-already disrupted for the subject by the traumatic cut inflicted by the symbolic, is no more than myth, '*pure imagination*', but 'imagination at its most violent' (1999a: 33). This mythic, chaotic real, the 'monstrous' real-in-fragments, as depicted by Hieronymus Bosch and the Surrealists, represents 'the impossible moment' of the birth of a subject determined by the death drive (52).

Jouissance, the encounter with the real, is always traumatic. The horrifying impossible-possibility of directly experiencing the 'something missing' from the 'In-itself' (1997: 179) is screened by the symbolic order, a place of fantasy which enables the subject to support the otherwise unbearable encounter with the real. Physical sexual contact with another human being is inherently traumatic, and that is why it has to be masked by fantasy (1997: 65). In this context Žižek does differentiate the *objet a* at the level of demand from the unrepresentable real (1997: 2, 64–5). But the fantasy commonly resembles the absent materiality it is designed to conceal, so that he finds the real made manifest in the giant sea-beast of cinematic imagination, putrefied flesh, or the visceral rubberiness of the Hollywood Alien. In one instance, it takes the form of the shimmering, pulsatile sphere that vibrates with a kind of life in Barry Levinson's film *Sphere* (1998). The sphere itself is empty, and yet it endows the protagonists with the capacity to materialize their own worst and most destructive fears. We should understand, Žižek argues, that 'as Real, as the impossible Thing, the Sphere is an entity of *pure semblance*' (Žižek 1999a: 302). The real is no more than a copy of itself; it has no existence independent of the social reality where its representation appears.

Žižek thus reduces Lacan's three levels to two. Where Lacan identifies the organism, the symbolic and the unconscious, Žižek reinstates a binary opposition between social reality, on the one hand, which includes the semblance of the real and, on the other, the terrain of the drive, where there is nothing but the void of the real itself. Behind the veil for Lacan, the fruitless search for the *objet a* that takes the place of the lost real; behind the veil for Žižek, the traumatic encounter with the monstrous real, which is nothing but the phantasmic actualization of our own desire (1999a: 302).

By contrast, Lacan's real, non-mythic, unconstructed, cannot be encountered at any level. In the seminar on the *tuché*, the (missed) encounter, he insists that the father wakes up rather than dream the death of his son: such recognition, even unconsciously, is intolerable even there. But it cannot be acknowledged in the symbolic either, because 'no one can say what the death of a child is except the father *qua* father, that is to say, no conscious being'. Even unconsciously, even in the dream, the father avoids the inextricable, unnameable real of that intimate, organic bond (Lacan 1979: 59, 68).

Žižek's formulations lead me to believe that he would not, if pressed, deny the existence of brute 'things', any more than Hegel does. But the real in this sense is of no interest, because it is not there for *a subject*. What matters to Žižek is the retroactively constructed element of the real subsumed by the speaking, acting, traumatized and thus quintessentially aggressive human being.

What matters to us, I might add, in Žižek's own work, is its philosophical range, its independence, its insights into popular culture and, above all, the politics of its account of antagonism rooted in the death drive. I have stressed what I see as his difference from Lacan at the moments when he claims to be most Lacanian because my argument is not in the first instance with his theory of human nature, but rather with the idealism it seems to involve. As far as I can see, Žižek's account of aggressivity, and of the successive hate-objects produced to screen the absence at the heart of the symbolic order, would be perfectly compatible with a non-idealist Lacan. Of course, Žižek does not share Hegel's optimistic belief in a rational consciousness that perfectly matches the world. But by identifying the real with the void, he reaffirms, contrary to Lacan, the idealist view that determination is exercised not by the world but only by our idea of it, conscious or unconscious.

IMAGINARY SOVEREIGNTY

Why, in more general terms, should we worry about idealism? Or, to put it differently, what has cultural criticism to gain by invoking the Lacanian real? As Žižek rightly points out, the mysterious form in *Sphere* materializes the contents of people's psyches. But this remarkable object belongs to science fiction. Lacan, in contrast, offers an independent material alterity: 'the real is what does not depend on my idea of it' (Fink 1995: 142). Which account has more to offer cultural critics?

'What could it possibly mean', Lacan asks early on, 'to say that the subject is everything?' (1988b: 98). What indeed? Perfect sovereignty for the subject, damaged or not, of course. Idealism delivers what the free West prizes most. In a world without alterity, I increasingly constitute my own origin; moreover, I construct my own body, cause my own diseases by bad habits or irrational worry, and bring about my own death if I am foolish enough to let either of these get out of hand. Western culture treats life as a constant process of self-fashioning, unimpeded by external constraints. In science fiction Hollywood heroes materialize their anxieties; in cultural theory I materialize my own sex.

Death, however, remains frightening, as does the threat of physical impairment that would impugn our autonomy. Idealism turns the object of desire into an increasingly prosthetic immortality, secured by remorseless self-discipline: a regime of diet and exercise, supplemented by surgery.

Lacan saw the possibility of assuming our own being-for-death as heroic, the consequence of a struggle to be what we are in the face of everything that may oppose us. His Antigone asserts her autonomy against the cultural script, and against the 'good sense' of other people, who urge her not to break the law. Idealism, by contrast, leaves such autonomy there for the taking, or rules it out on the basis of cultural determinism. In the absence of any substantial alterity, how or what should we oppose? The abolition of opposition in turn does away with the heroism.

Žižek, aware of the seductions of imaginary sovereignty, repeatedly insists that we should 'traverse the fantasy' presented by the symbolic order, go through the cultural screen to encounter the emptiness beyond it (1997: 30–31). This bleak proposition takes Lacan's account of the death drive to its logical conclusion, but it is his subscription to idealism in the first place that makes it all the more imperative for Žižek to prescribe suicide as the supreme ethical act. Traversing the fantasy to the void both constitutes a counterweight to the self-indulgence of an idealist culture, and at the same time installs the true sovereignty of the subject itself (see, for example, 1991: 63–4; 1992a: 77–8).

VIOLENCE

If the subject constitutes its own origin, what about the world the subject inhabits? Idealism ultimately devalues all that resides outside our own heads. That idealist complacency, the certainty that we not only make ourselves, but also make the world in our own minds, confining what exists to consciousness and erasing the real in the process, may be one of the most dangerous features of Western culture in the twenty-first century. To the degree that we ourselves are at our own disposal, so too is the rest of the world, to make of it whatever we choose. While idealism does not overtly ally itself with the West's depredation of the planet or its militaristic foreign policy, a theory that materiality is no more than the effect of culture offers no grounds for repudiating either of these practices. On the contrary, the conviction that what exists depends on our idea of it helps to disconnect our lifestyle from the damage it causes.

Meanwhile, our warfare is conducted at a distance, at 30,000 feet, and on computer screens, while statistics replace the real of suffering bodies. Battles are relayed to non-combatants on television, where grand firework displays largely filter out the death and mutilation they bring about. Thereafter, endless talking heads recount, discuss, analyse, pore over and debate the details of what has not been shown. In that sense, idealism surely supports a society ready to ignore the vulnerable organisms that people also are, as well as the destruction our armies can inflict in the name of an idea.

Jean Baudrillard drew attention to this 'triumph of the virtual over the real' in his response to the first Gulf War in 1991 (1995: 50). We are naive, he argued in The Gulf War Did Not Take Place, if we expect to learn the truth about wars, or demand the 'proper' use of information as a record of what actually happens (46–7). The event, he comments, in a particularly Hegelian moment, vanishes in the information itself (47). But we should not blame error, or inadequate reporting. The first Gulf War was hardly a war at all, since there was no Iraqi resistance. But that, after all, was the point: the 'war' was about the display of Western firepower and the impossibility of effective resistance. It was a spectacle designed to deter, shown in electronic space and for the benefit of the world at large.

Baudrillard infers from this analysis that we should not be fooled. Instead, we should recognize what is at stake, without succumbing to the illusion that we are being informed:

> Be more virtual than events themselves, do not seek to re-establish the truth, we do not have the means, but do not be duped, and to that end re-immerse the war and all the information in the virtuality from whence they come. Turn deterrence back against itself.
>
> (66–7)

The Gulf War Did Not Take Place has been widely and unjustly caricatured, usually on the basis of its title alone, but it offers more insight than its detractors acknowledge. On the other hand, Baudrillard's thinking is characteristically binary, and in consequence less sophisticated than it might appear. Reversing the conventional hierarchy, affirming the virtual over the truth, he simply brackets the real, the actuality of mutilation and death. Not included in the information we are given, by definition unknowable, the real goes unmentioned.

Jacques Derrida comments on the limitations of this binary thinking in an interview conducted in 1994. Though he does not explicitly mention Baudrillard, Derrida warns against the easy inference that war is reducible to a media spectacle. We may not know the truth as such, but it would be equally naive to suppose that that leaves us with nothing but fiction. 'Clearly,' Derrida concedes, 'it is no longer possible to contrast virtuality with actual reality, along the lines of the serene old philosophical distinction'. But he also warns against the consequent disavowal of what takes place, against

> a denial of events, by which everything – even violence and suffering, war and death – is said to be constructed and fictive, and constituted by and for the media, so that nothing ever really happens, only images, simulacra, and delusions. The deconstruction of artifactuality should be carried as far as possible, but we must also take every precaution against this kind of critical neo-idealism. We must bear in mind ... that any coherent deconstruction is about singularity, about events, and about what is ultimately irreducible in them.
>
> (Derrida 1994: 29)

THE INCURSION OF THE REAL

There is some evidence, however, that the irreducible real is beginning to put up a resistance to our wasteful, culturally scripted habits, and to make itself knowable in the form of melting icecaps, floods, forest fires and high levels of skin cancer. Sadly, the West, which has done most to bring this about, only grudgingly acknowledges the situation, at least explicitly, while at the same time scrambling for control of the planet's remaining natural resources.

Meanwhile, events are reasserting their own singularity. On 11 September 2001 two planes flew into the twin towers of the World Trade Center in New York, killing some 3,000 people. This occurrence was appalling, tragic, but no more so, it might be argued, than the Western bombing of cities in other parts of the world at intervals since the Second World War. It left, however, a deep wound. The event proved unnameable, except by its date, and led to military reprisals on a huge scale, first in Afghanistan and then in Iraq.

Why was 9/11 so shocking? Perhaps because it represented the momentary incursion of the unknowable real into an increasingly idealist culture. The destruction of the twin towers seemed unheralded, inexplicable, unaccountable, out of our control. In the immediate aftermath of the event, sophisticated commentators, including Žižek, delighted in maintaining that 9/11 was first and foremost a media spectacle, reproducing in actuality an already-familiar Hollywood fantasy.[1]

But while the television images have gradually faded, the repercussions of the event have shown that the scar goes deeper. We watch disaster movies from choice, and admire them as a display of American cinematic skill. By contrast, 9/11 impugned the sovereignty of America's defences and the reliability of Western intelligence. More than this, however, it also called into question the West's whole world picture, our sense of our own ability to write the script. These planes were not a repressed fragment of our own psyche but, on the contrary, a violent material intrusion from outside. Idealism could not accommodate them.

LACAN AGAINST IDEALISM

Lacan himself resolutely and consistently opposed idealism, which he called the 'extreme of vertigo' (1979: 71). Psychoanalysis, he insisted, does not lead in that direction (1979: 53). Instead, it turns on 'the signifier's relations with the real', and both these terms carry their own weight. But each of them has implications for the other. Although he concedes that 'the signifier marks the real as much and more than it represents it', he adds, 'Don't be mistaken. There's no idealism in this' (1990: 76).

Social reality offers gratifications, but these do not quite match up with unconscious desire. In that sense, for Lacan social reality is no more than a fantasy. Does he, then, deny the existence of the material world after all, reproducing a version of idealism in spite of himself? It can sound like it. For instance, in Seminar 20 he urges that: 'The world, the world of the being full of knowledge, is but a dream, a dream of the body insofar as it speaks, for there's no such thing as a knowing subject' (1998: 126; translation modified in the light of 1975: 114). The dream here, however, is not the world itself, but the claim to know, the deluded certainty of the being full of knowledge, for there is no such thing as a knowing subject, but only subjects who have learned what their culture knows, or seems to know.

Since there is no such thing as a knowing subject, however, the claim that the world does not exist, or the certainty that only ideas are real, is just as much a dream in Lacan's view. Paradoxically, to deny the real is also to claim to know for sure. The subject can never achieve such surety, the correspondence between world and consciousness that was Hegel's goal. Nor can it confidently assert even the more modest conviction that what we don't know doesn't matter. How can we be sure even of that, when we can be certain of nothing?

On the contrary, while he was fully aware of idealism's seductive appeal, its promise of an assured knowledge for the subject, Lacan himself was not seduced:

> Idealism consists in affirming that we are the ones who give shape to reality, and that there is no point in looking any further. It is a

comfortable position. Freud's position, or that of any sensible man for that matter, is something very different.

(1992: 30)

What idealism misses, he maintains, is the crucial contribution of psychoanalysis, its understanding of the continuity between the subject and the world, interrupted but not finally erased by the advent of the symbolic order. We remain marked by the lost but inextricable real. The subject is alienated by the Otherness of the signifier and the consequent lack in being, with its propensity at any moment to subtract something from coherent thought or speech. We are subject to temporary disappearances from the signifying chain, liable at any moment to *fade*. Indeed,

> this is the essential flaw in philosophical idealism which, in any case, cannot be sustained and has never been radically sustained. There is no subject without, somewhere, *aphanisis* [fading] of the subject, and it is in this alienation, in this fundamental division, that the dialectic of the subject is established.

(1979: 221)

The speaking being cannot fully apprehend its own condition, composed, as it is, of a subjectivity that uneasily inhabits an inaccessible, unnameable real. Not simply mind or body, nor even mind *and* body, such a creature is always other than it is. 'Mind' – or language and culture – comes in the first instance from outside the subject in an effort to name the organic imperatives that this alien demand never fully matches.

Does the psychoanalytic account of the distinction between the social reality we construct and the unknowable real revert, then, to Kant's opposition between appearances and things-in-themselves? Yes and no. Lacan repudiates – deconstructs, in practice, though he does not, of course, use the word – the Kantian antithesis between what we cannot know and the phenomena we perceive. Human beings are not, Lacan insists, *paraîtres*, or mere appearances, but *par-êtres*, para-beings, taking up a position as subjects alongside another condition, from which the signifier always alienates us. We are, in other words, perpetually beside ourselves (1998: 44–5).

With this deconstruction of the antithesis between mind and body, thought and world, symbolic and real, psychoanalysis replaces an opposition which otherwise would require us to take sides. Bishop Berkeley could not be sure that things were still there when we were not looking at them. Asked how he would counter such idealism, Dr Johnson replied, 'I refute it thus', and kicked a stone. Since then, much theory has either opted to travel some way along the lines laid down by German idealism, or else rejected 'continental philosophy' in its entirety in favour of an uncomplicated empiricism. Lacan, by contrast, challenges mind–body dualism, allowing for the invasion of the signifier into the real, at the same time as the violent incursion of the real event into a world-picture not designed to recognize it. Psychoanalysis takes as its specific field of interest the enigma that issues from the unstable conjunction of the two in human beings. 'The real . . . is the mystery of the speaking body, the mystery of the unconscious' (Lacan 1998: 131).

CULTURE

At the same time, Lacan promises a degree of consolation for the alienated, enigmatic figure, perpetually beside itself, that his rereading of Freud makes of the speaking subject. Lacan's view of culture, paradoxically, turns out to be much more positive than any account the constructivists offer. According to new historicism, culture polices even our dissent; Butler's cultural script inscribes sexual oppression with only a very limited possibility of resistance; Fish's corrals us into interpretive communities, where if we disagree, all we can do is go elsewhere. In Žižek's account, meanwhile, cultural life is peopled by phantasmic objects of fear and loathing. Lacan, by contrast, sees culture as the location of pleasure.

In the rest of this book, I shall be concerned with the forms of this pleasure, and the implications for cultural criticism of acknowledging the determinations exerted by the unknowable real.

5

CULTURE'S MAGIC CIRCLE

THE REAL AND CULTURE

The signifier and the real exist on different levels. True, the signifier invades the unknown spaces of the real in the construction of new knowledges, while the real now and then forces its way violently into the cultural reality we make for ourselves. But do the distinct levels remain in the normal course of things separate and mutually antagonistic, culture struggling to paper over a gap in the symbolic that it can never close?

Yes and no. The burial of the dead, I have suggested, is among the most ancient of cultural practices. Memorials to the dead acknowledge on the plane of the signifier the capacity of the real to reclaim the subject. Mounds, pyramids, monuments all mark the existence of a former speaking being who has now rejoined the real. A presence testifies to an absence. Tombs set out to immortalize an individual, but without denying, paradoxically, the loss of the person that they are also designed to overcome.

Suppose, then, we consider in the first instance a specific funeral monument as an example of culture. I have deliberately chosen the memorial to a figure we now know almost nothing about, in order not to confuse the tomb with its occupant, or to be side-tracked by biography. Inscriptions and effigies invite us to speculate about their subjects, of course, and this one is no exception. But exactly because our knowledge remains at the level of speculation, we are in a stronger position to focus on the way commemoration works as a cultural form.

JOHN SIMSON, APOTHECARY

Entrance to the parish church of St Mary, Debenham is still through the west door. Though the base of the tower dates back to the eleventh century, the Perpendicular south aisle is well lit, and there is no difficulty in distinguishing the figure of John Simson, apothecary, whose three-quarter image is turned slightly in its niche at the west end of the south wall to face parishioners as they come into the church. Simson's left hand touches his breast in a gesture of sorrow, or perhaps pity, but the right is raised in greeting or blessing. The missing thumb and little finger, cleanly broken off, do not detract from the melancholy authority that has evidently characterized his effigy since it was commissioned on or soon after his death in 1697 by his close friend, John Sheppard, Clerk to the neighbouring parish of Wetheringsett-cum-Brockford (Figure 5.1).

The tomb of this obscure seventeenth-century apothecary, neither magnificent nor conventionally beautiful, but engaging none the less, testifies to loss, invoking signifying practice to immortalize its subject. But immortality, at least in this world, is not an option for John Simson; death is real. In place of eternal life, however, the monument presents a cultural 'text' which at once alludes to loss and promises pleasure. In this respect, memorial sculpture constitutes a paradigm instance of culture as Lacanian psychoanalysis defines it.

The family of John Sheppard, who set up Simson's tomb, was of some consequence in this part of rural Suffolk. They were entitled to bear arms: three hounds holding arrows in their mouths, with the inscription, '*Dat tela fidelitas*' ('Faithfulness provides weapons'). John Simson, however, belonged to a different social class. Although Simson's portrait bust was conventionally appropriate to a professional man, the status of apothecaries at the end of the seventeenth

Figure 5.1 John Simson greets parishioners in Debenham, Suffolk.
(Monument to John Simson, d. 1697, detail of tomb.)

century remained low. They were tradesmen, held in some contempt
even by the emerging medical profession, itself not yet highly
regarded. If Shakespeare exaggerated their destitution in the figure
who sells Romeo the poison, apothecaries in the late seventeenth
century were still not entirely respectable. They were entitled to
charge for medicines at this time, but not for advice, in case they
should encroach on the territory claimed by physicians. Nor, therefore, were they accustomed to expect a monument laying claim to
such visibility. It was John Sheppard's family arms that appeared on
the marble tablet below the figure of John Simson, with a Latin
inscription testifying to Sheppard's responsibility for designing the
tomb of his dearly beloved friend.

And yet Sheppard's design invested the apothecary with the dignity
of his own coat of arms, even so. The carving on the black basalt
lid of the tomb-chest includes a helmet above a shield that shows a
cross, a crown of thorns and two reeds, identified as 'the insignia
of any Christian'. Simson's arms are the shield of faith and the helmet

of salvation (Ephesians 6, 16–17). An accompanying poem in English, composed, presumably, by Sheppard himself, explains that the emblems evident on the shield lay no claim to a noble genealogy for the dead man: 'We boast not here (kind reader) a descent/From Brittish, Saxon, or the Norman race.' Instead, they symbolize the humility of Christ's Passion:

> Thus here those instruments of shame and paine,
> Which our Dear Lord for man did not disdaine;
> Of honourable arms we in the room
> Display, true ensigns for a Christians tomb.
>   Such Heraldry as this let none despise,
>   Free from the Censure of the good and wise.

This attribution to the apothecary of a nobility that belongs to virtue, regardless of birth, is consistent with the elaborate character of the monument itself. The niche proclaims Simson's faith, hope and charity, exhorting the viewer in Latin, 'So let your light shine' (Matthew 5, 16). Two urns indicate his death ('*Extinguor*') and ultimate resurrection ('*Resurgam*'). Below these, English verses assert the hope of eternal life faith promises, and urge spectators to trim their lamps in readiness, like the wise virgins in the parable (Matthew 25, 1–13).

DEATH AND THE SIGNIFIER

The portrait-bust, the wealth of familiar allegorical symbols and allusions, as well as inscriptions in English, Latin and Greek, combine to memorialize the humble apothecary. Almost every available signifying practice joins forces here against the annihilating power of death. The monument not only affirms his immortality, but does its best to confer it too, making John Simson live in durable stone, both a personal friend to John Sheppard and a moral example to succeeding generations.

And yet to formulate in these terms the immortalizing project of the tomb, and, indeed, of all memorial sculpture, is to make clear in the process the impossibility of the task. Nothing, in one sense, could be further from the presence of the living being than the allegory inscribed in this fixed and unyielding stone. The geometry, the regularity of the tablet itself, the antithetical disposition of the urns, the plethora of emblems and the verbal inscriptions in languages either living or dead, but always formal, whether testamentary, scriptural, proverbial or heroic, all betray, in spite of themselves, precisely their own incapacity to bring the dead man to breathing life. Any effigy draws attention by its cold stillness to the difference between monumentality on the one hand, and the flesh and blood of a living organism on the other. Here the gap between the apothecary and his memorial is only emphasized by the elaboration of the visual signifiers, the flurry of textuality and the static symmetry, all of them necessary, just the same, in the interests of the projected commemoration itself.

Nor does the dead man's flesh and blood apparently live in his descendants. While monumental inscriptions to the gentry in this period characteristically focus on lines of descent, the tombs of scholars and professionals more commonly emphasize their achievements. There is no allusion to a family anywhere on the memorial that embraces such a wealth of signifiers. Large and slightly mournful marble putti on either side of the mimetic effigy are explicitly emblematic. 'I was hungry', announces the child on the left with the sheaf of corn; 'I was naked', adds the little boy on the right holding the edges of a cloak. Their utterances allude to the Last Judgement, when Christ will reward those who fed the hungry and clothed the destitute (Matthew 25, 35–46). The claim of the putti is borne out by a detailed account in Latin on the side of the tomb-chest. As apothecary to a small Suffolk market-town, John Simson seems to have made enough money by the time he died at the age of fifty-four to institute in perpetuity a weekly distribution of bread to forty poor people on Sundays at the end of morning service, and an annual allocation of clothes to fourteen of the poorest parishioners every Christmas Day. He thus constitutes an example, the inscription concludes, of generous and well-organized charity.

It is tempting to wonder about the precise nature of the relationship between Simson, the apothecary, and the landowner, Sheppard, who commissioned the monument. John Sheppard lived five miles away in the parish of Wetheringsett. He was baptized there in January 1649/50, so he would have been some seven years younger than his friend. Simson's charitable bequests may, perhaps, offer a clue to the character of their shared interests. It was possible for tradesmen to enhance their social status by involvement in alms-giving. John Sheppard made a will in 1707, ten years after the apothecary's death, which resembles Simson's very closely. Sheppard's estates were to provide twopenny loaves for six of the poor every Sunday after the service. Moreover, he left a small plot of land called Church Pightle to cover the cost of an annual feast for twenty poor people of Wetheringsett on the festival of the Annunciation in March. The parson was to read prayers before dinner, the ringers to provide a peal of bells afterwards, and the poor were to receive sixpence each in addition. Sheppard was extremely specific about the distri-bution of the money. The food would cost one pound; five shillings would go to the cook, two shillings and sixpence to the Parson and another two and sixpence to the ringers. He thus offered a further example of the generous and well-ordered charity he had praised on the side of his friend's tomb. The main difference is that the gentleman posthumously invited the poor to dinner, while the prudent apothe-cary, who would have known the value of preventive medicine, left clothes to keep them warm.

Both men, then, will live on in their bequests, and in the gratitude of their beneficiaries. And yet, after his own generation, it is hard to believe that the poor, however grateful, will conjure up, as they receive their Sunday bread and their Christmas clothing, even so much as an image of the living John Simson. What survives instead is a fund administered in their interests, and the textuality of a seventeenth-century will. The monument names Simson's skill as an apothecary and his Christian virtues, as well as the love of his friend, John Sheppard. The remainder, the real of the organism, and the nature of the friendship, remains unnameable, inaccessible to the signifier, lost and relegated beyond reach by the very monument designed to preserve his memory.

CULTURE AND THE THING

Monuments depend, in other words, on the existence of a gap between the real and the symbolic. The loss they set out to erase by preserving a memory, the death it is their project to overcome by this means, is also the condition of their existence as objects in culture. John Simson's monument alludes to the death it also seeks to overcome. Designed to house his remains, it will contain decomposition, bones and then dust. The hollow tomb that is to immortalize the apothecary comes to conceal more or less nothing – and offers a compensating, consoling pleasure. In Lacanian terms, tombs form a magic circle round the Thing.

We glimpsed the Thing in Chapter 3 as the predecessor of the *objet a*. This construct makes itself felt only briefly in the course of Lacan's work, possibly because it hovers uneasily between the real and the symbolic, but it features prominently in *Seminar 7* (1992), where Lacan gives his most detailed account of culture. For that reason, I now return to the Thing (*das Ding*) in slightly more detail. While Lacan locates the Thing in the real, it inhabits the psyche, as the real does not, though it appears there as a kind of exile. The object of an unnameable desire, the Thing does not exist as such, except as a psychic reminder, but marks the place in the speaking being of the lost real, and thus introduces emptiness into continuity. Beyond the signifier, alien to the subject, the Thing also constitutes the absence that appears at the heart of the subject with the advent of signification. An archaic, maternal construct from the subject's prehistory, the unforgettable Thing is the source of an impulsion towards life and death, the (non-existent) object of the single drive that comprehends both.

As the nothing at the centre of the speaking being, the Thing is what we unconsciously want in the lost real. But it can never be found, Lacan insists. On the contrary, the subject must keep its distance from the Thing. Too close an encounter, he affirms, even supposing it were possible, would bring about the dissolution of the subject, the symbolic order and culture in its entirety.

But its converse, the Law, conscience, the order represented by the symbolic Father, offers no satisfaction either. As Lacan's appropriation of the Freudian superego, the Father in Lacan's account is consistently dead, a 'morbid' tyrant whose demands for renunciation are insatiable, exorbitant. Like the Thing, the Law is a stranger, but it is also the source of an 'obscene and ferocious' jurisdiction (1992: 7).

Conscience is a 'parasite' that feeds on the satisfactions we give it and still demands more (89). Lacan contemptuously dismisses its ethical values of self-sacrifice, duty and discipline as 'the goods'.

There is no 'Sovereign Good'. Instead, the forbidden, deadly Thing is also the source of good, and 'there is no other' (70). Since Lacan joins Freud's two imperatives of desire and death in a single drive, the object of the drive, the maternal Thing gives life as well as death. Hostile to the subject (52), and yet 'on its side' (1986: 125), the Thing constitutes the source of love and hate alike, its place both living and dead (300). It thus initiates the will to create as well as destroy – to destroy, indeed, Lacan argues, in order to create anew.

Creativity is the project of culture. By this means, culture offers a detour that keeps the Thing itself at bay, defers with its own signi-fying presence the impossible *jouissance* of the encounter with pure absence, and gives pleasure in the process. Lacan sees cultural objects as encircling the lost Thing, keeping it within bounds, without denying its existence. Funeral monuments go back a long way as a paradigm instance of culture. John Simson's surrounds absence with the signifier, and offers a certain pleasure as it does so.

PLEASURE

As Freud points out in *Beyond the Pleasure Principle*, and Lacan reiterates, pleasure for the subject is to be found on the side of the symbolic, not the real (Lacan 1992: 12). The object of the drive, the Thing, missing from the symbolic, outside representation, absent, is both inconceivable and terrifying. But the symbolic order, which in the first instance divorced the human infant from gratification in the real, goes on to form a 'magic circle', which separates us from the Thing (134). Little Ernst replaced the organic connection to his mother with the signifying wooden reel, and thus came to accept her absences. But it is important to note that, while this process named the pain of absence, it did not do away with it. It is in the context of this story that Freud mentions the artistic pleasures of grown-ups. These often incorporate loss at the level of the signifier, he points out. His instance is tragedy, which dramatizes suffering and death, and yet may be experienced as enjoyable (Freud 1984: 287).

The pleasure principle does not repress the drive, but deflects it, imposing the signifying screen that protects us from a direct encounter with the desired, impossible, deadly Thing. At the same time, the pleasurable signifier alludes to its loss. Even comedy, from Shakespeare to *Four Weddings and a Funeral*, notoriously also recognizes the dark side of human experience. The pleasure principle is aligned with culture in the broadest sense of that term.

THE BEAUTIFUL

Culture consists in making things. It thus gratifies that element of the death drive that is intelligible as a will to start again, to erase in order to recreate, to make something out of the nothing that destruction produces (Lacan 1992: 212). The works of culture may be no more than fictions, hallucinated satisfactions that gratify at an imaginary level. Alternatively, they may be to varying degrees beautiful, in the Kantian sense of the term, which is to say satisfying, pleasurable, and in consequence disarming. The beautiful satisfies, Lacan argues, to the degree that it does, not by representing the real, nor by avoiding the drive, but instead by pointing to the lost real, while at the same time fencing off any possibility that we might come too close to the Thing. Made objects offer a kind of satisfaction when the signifier encloses absence and at the same time offers pleasure.

Architecture takes form by encircling emptiness (1992: 135–6); art creates a signifying surface that supplants its model; the theme of mourning for an impossible object of desire dominates the poetry of the troubadours (139–54). Much love poetry centres on absence. Tragedy paradoxically offers its audience not despair at the death of the hero, but consolation in the form of catharsis. And tombs, though Lacan does not mention them, enclose the void. John Simson's monument decorates the screen it constitutes with texts and images that evoke his life. In all these cases, the allusion to absence, the construction of something out of nothing, and the reference to the nothing which is the condition of that construction, all combine to offer a kind of satisfaction by pacifying the drive.

Rereading Heidegger's essay, 'The Origin of the Work of Art', Lacan cites as an instance of the beautiful Van Gogh's sequence of

Figure 5.2 A pair of abandoned clodhoppers indicate a presence and an absence. (Vincent van Gogh, *A Pair of Shoes*, 1887.)

paintings of *A Pair of Shoes* (Figure 5.2). What gratification can we derive from images of the footwear a peasant has discarded? Where is the pleasure in a painting of these clumsy, graceless and worn shoes, he wonders. What, after all, do they *mean*? Not walking, not fatigue; neither passion nor a human relationship. On the contrary, he continues, they mean no more than 'that which is signified by a pair of abandoned clodhoppers, namely, both a presence and a pure absence' (1992: 297). No one wears these shoes: they are empty. They thus indicate a temporal relationship, a difference from the past, a loss of the wearer, just as a wooden reel symbolizes the loss of the organic relationship with a beloved mother.

In the same way, a still life implies a temporal relationship with the future, a potential for loss there too. Milk or fruit, cream, oranges or grapes, depicted at a moment of perfection, depend for the pleasure they give on our awareness that the moment can't last.

As Claudel showed so admirably in his study of Dutch painting, it is to the extent that the still life both reveals and hides that within

> it which constitutes a threat, denouement, unfolding, or decompos-
> ition, that it manifests the beautiful for us as a function of a temporal
> relation.
>
> (298)

That ambiguity is critical. Art, signifying form, at once both constitutes a presence and invokes absence. In Derridean terms, the signifier,
which defers meaning, takes its place. In this way, it represents the
absence it invokes, paradoxically makes what is not there evident
in presentation itself; a work of art draws attention to the immi-
nence of death, and it does so in signifying practice. The work thus
protects the viewer from the impossible experience, annihilating for
the subject, of absence as such.

> The true barrier that holds the subject back in front of the unspeak-
> able field of radical desire that is the field of absolute destruction
> ... is properly speaking the aesthetic phenomenon where it is
> identified with the experience of beauty.
>
> (216–17)

Does the satisfaction culture affords depend on beauty in the
conventional sense, the kind of beauty we identify with high culture?
Not necessarily. The archetypal cultural object, Lacan argues, is the
work of the potter, who creates a space by making a vase to surround
it (120–21). And here he echoes another of Heidegger's essays.
What *holds* the liquid in a jug, Heidegger asks. Not, as it might appear,
the sides and floor of the jug. On the contrary, the indispensable
element is the hole at the centre. 'The emptiness, the void, is what
does the vessel's holding. The empty space, this nothing of the
jug, is what the jug is as the holding vessel.' The potter 'shapes the
void' (Heidegger 1971: 169). And Heidegger adds, since only human
beings are aware of death, and specifically their own mortality, 'Death
is the shrine of Nothing' (178).

Lacan appropriates Heidegger's interpretation of the potter's work
for his own specifically psychoanalytic account of culture. Whenever
the signifier makes a magic circle round the absent Thing, we are
entitled to find a kind of beauty. In a certain context, a collection
of empty matchboxes encloses and inscribes the lost real (Lacan 1992:

114). Lacan calls Little Ernst's toy a *cotton-reel* (1979: 62), thereby introducing, whether deliberately or not, a hole through its centre. Even macaroni, as a hole with pasta round it, constitutes an elementary cultural object: and here too the fashioning culture performs introduces a gap or a void into the continuity of the real (121); it both creates and encircles emptiness.

Even though Lacan does not mention it, then, monumental sculpture, the signifier surrounding a loss, whether or not it meets the highest standards of beauty, constitutes a paradigm case of the pleasure that pacifies the drive.

TEXTUALITY

As the living being he once was, John Simson cannot be made present in his memorial, but something of the philanthropic apothecary survives in his monument, which is not altogether beautiful in the conventional sense, but remains oddly pleasurable, none the less. The inscriptions record the virtues of a subject in culture, a skilful chemist who did not know, ironically, how to prescribe his own health, at the mercy, we learn, of a persistent disease which was beyond his own art and also that of Aesculapius, god of healing. Simson determined, therefore, to give the poor a better life, we are told, since he could not prolong his own or anyone else's.

What was he like, this benevolent and sensible small-town pharmacist, we may want in vain to know. And what was the character of his friendship with the gentleman-Clerk to the adjacent Parish, who devoted so much care and attention to the wealth of signification that records John Simson's exemplary virtues? Eight years earlier, in 1689, John Sheppard had installed a tomb slab in the chancel at Wetheringsett in memory of his own parents, John and Susan. The black marble rectangle is plain, elegant and minimalist, perhaps Puritan. Below the Sheppard family coat of arms, a prose inscription records the learning, piety, prudence and faith of his father, as well as his excellent relations with other people, and the warmth and courtesy of his mother, Susan.

What emotion, then, motivated the elaborate allegories, as well as the mimetic representation, and the textuality in three languages, in both prose and verse, that Sheppard incorporated into the Simson monument? John Simson's will, still available for consultation in the Public Record Office, offers a tantalizing glimpse of the context. In the first place, trade must have been good. The will records a number of purchases of land, so that by the time he died Simson was able to identify himself as a gentleman, and leave a good deal of property, as well as many minor bequests. Second, there is no evidence that he ever married. His main beneficiary was his cousin, another John Simson (or Simpson), himself the son of an apothecary of Diss, Norfolk. And finally, Simson himself evidently had a hand in the design of his monument:

> Item my desire is that my loveing friend John Sheppard of Weatheringsett Gent doe affix such a Tombe Stone as he and I have often discoursed of to be putt upon the south side of Debenham church in the most convenient place at his discretion.

How detailed were these frequent discussions? How much was left to Sheppard's discretion? What was Simson's motive? Immortality for himself? For social mobility? For good works? And what was Sheppard's? Moral instruction? Or a testament to a loving friendship?

Our desire to look behind the veil, in conjunction with the fact that our curiosity cannot be gratified, goes to emphasize the temporal gap that is paradoxically both the motive for immortalization and the major obstacle to its achievement. Like Van Gogh's painted shoes, John Sheppard's testament to his dead friend indicates at the level of the signifier an absence that marks the trace of a presence.

Along the base of the tomb-chest a Greek inscription quotes 2 Timothy, 1.18: 'The Lord grant unto him that he may find mercy of the Lord in that day.' The reference here is to the Last Judgement, when Christ will assign the risen dead to everlasting life in heaven or to their final separation from God in the desolation of hell. But Sheppard – or Simson, or both – had evidently given the choice of quotation some thought. The selection of this specific text implies a further allusion to Simson's good deeds. The biblical verse goes on, 'and in how many things he ministered unto me at Ephesus, thou knowest very well'. His friend, Onesiphorus, St Paul records in this chapter, has not turned from him, like so many. On the contrary, 'he oft refreshed me', and 'when he was in Rome, he sought me out very diligently, and found me' (16–17).

Sheppard has clearly done everything in his power to render his friend's kindness eternal at the level of the signifier, not only in this world, but also in the face of the Judgement that will determine his participation in the life to come.

A SHAKESPEARE SONNET

A century earlier, Shakespeare's Sonnet 55 is scathing about the ability of 'marble' and 'gilded monuments' to immortalize their subjects. Even so, like many of the *Sonnets*, this text affirms in its own way the capacity of culture to preserve the life of the dead. In place of the repudiated monumental 'masonry' and 'statues' (the meaning of the word included effigies at that time), Sonnet 55 offers 'this powerful rhyme'. Not a tomb, this time, but the poem itself, as 'The living record of your memory', promises its addressee survival until the Last Day:

> 'Gainst death, and all oblivious enmity,
> Shall you pace forth; your praise shall still find room
> Even in the eyes of all posterity
> That wear this world out to the ending doom.
>   So till the judgement that yourself arise,
>   You live in this, and dwell in lovers' eyes.

The claim of Sonnet 55 to bridge the gap between death and the final resurrection invokes the traditional form of aristocratic tombs, where the figures face the east, their eyes open, in expectation of the Second Coming. In the chancel at Debenham lies the effigy of Sir Charles Framlingham, who died in 1595, probably close to the date of Shakespeare's *Sonnets*. Beside him, his wife is also placed horizontally along the tomb-chest, but her petticoats fall stiffly as if to the ground, while her feet are placed firmly at right-angles to their apparent resting place. Lady Framlingham's effigy is fully intelligible as a statue in the modern sense of the term, carved in the first instance as if she were standing, and then laid on its back to fit the space.[1] The hands of both figures are clasped in prayer.

It was the Victorians who represented their dead as asleep, or resting in peace until the Last Judgement. Earlier periods, by contrast, commonly imagined the subjects of monumental sculpture more actively seeking their own salvation in prayer or the works of virtue. John Sheppard's portrait bust of John Simson shows him alive, saluting parishioners, as perhaps he greeted the sick in his profession, or blessed the poor by deeds of alms.

In the way of love poems, Shakespeare's account of his friend goes one better, offering itself as a guarantee that its addressee will continue to 'pace forth' in stately and acknowledged indifference to the annihilation of death and oblivion. Taken literally, the claim invests poetry with miraculous powers. But even understood metaphorically, the promise has not been vindicated. We know still less about the addressee of the *Sonnets*, whether real or fictitious, than we do about the apothecary of Debenham a century later.

Like so many of Shakespeare's *Sonnets*, however, the poem equivocates concerning its central proposition. Is it the beloved, or the poem itself, that will live on? The immortality of the addressee is made conditional on the power of the 'rhyme' itself: 'you shall shine more bright in these contents/Than unswept stone, besmeared with sluttish time'; 'You live in this.'

What, then, is immortalized? 'You', or 'this'? The equivocation pervades the text. Which is the survivor here? ''Gainst death . . . /Shall you pace forth; your praise shall still find room.' Following so quickly after the words, 'Shall you pace', the phrase 'your praise shall', forms a kind of echo, almost but not quite reversing the sound pattern. Does the second phrase hastily take back the rash promise of a miracle, changing the contention even as it alters the word order? If so (and the tease is evidently not inadvertent), the claim that the praise, rather than the friend, will live on has been triumphantly vindicated by the prestige of the text four hundred years later. Shakespeare's *Sonnets* are not just on the syllabus; they are read out at weddings and funerals in many English-speaking countries; their rhythms and imagery remain familiar as part of the cultural repertoire of the Western world. Whatever their truth or fiction, whatever the fate of the addressee, and whatever the nature of the love inscribed in them, the *Sonnets* themselves survive, testifying to an emotion known only in its symbolic 'record', and familiar at the level of the signifier.

DEPREDATIONS

Shakespeare had a point about funeral monuments. 'Unswept stone', he called them in Sonnet 55, 'besmeared with sluttish time'. The stone that commemorates John Simson is currently very slightly unswept: I thought it best to brush away a few small spiders' webs to take his photograph. Sluttish time has also had its effects on his memorial. A finger and thumb, easily reachable from the conveniently placed tomb chest, have been neatly removed. A finial is missing from the urn on the right. The monument is now fenced off by spiked iron railings, perhaps to deter further depredations. Moreover, the wooden roof of the church has leaked directly overhead at some time, leaving brown stains on the marble tablet. And it took the expertise of Derek Hughes to decipher the contractions conventional in seventeenth-century Greek typography, but now generally forgotten. In spite of all that, however, the monument remains curiously moving as the inscription of a vanished friendship across class barriers and parish boundaries, and put to work not only in shared philanthropy but in the construction of an object in culture, a tomb that lavishes on its subject every possible kind of signifying attention.

Death is the inevitable fate of the human organism. John Simson's tomb does not deny that. But death is alien to the subject of Western culture, constituted as it is in the symbolic and divided in the process from the organism that we also are. Our languages, with their continuous present and their future tenses, enable us to imagine eternal life but, while culture survives (always subject, of course, to the effective control of weapons of mass destruction), the real withholds the possibility of immortality in this world for the individual human being. The monument, unable to make him present, alluding to loss and motivated by the annihilation of Simson himself, acknowledges that too. At the same time, however, it offers a certain consolation, in so far as it shares with *A Pair of Shoes* and Dutch painting, jugs, matchbox collections and macaroni the creation of a barrier to the experience, impossible for the subject, of pure absence. And perhaps, in its paradoxical signifying exuberance, the monument to the obscure apothecary also shares with all culture an existence as a pleasurable, pacifying alternative to renunciation, on the one hand, or aggressivity on the other.

6

MAKING SPACE

Perspective Vision and the Real

THE LIVING

Culture, like life, is for the living, however, and if in the last instance all culture inscribes an acknowledgement of death, the lonely hour of the last instance can seem a long way off. What relevance might the psychoanalytic account of culture have for the living? Not surprisingly, perhaps, culture has many ways to recognize and disarm the drive. Among these, the reproduction of perspective vision in painting, and subsequently in writing, hollows out a space to accommodate desire. The flat picture plane miraculously comes to simulate three dimensions, conjures depth of field, introducing the illusion of vacancy into the continuity of the real. And in the course of time, illusionist fiction followed suit. We are now so surrounded by high-resolution photography and film that the miracle of fixed-point perspective is easily taken for granted, with the effect of rendering imperceptible its relation to unconscious desire. But photography simply completes a programme inaugurated six centuries ago and elaborated in detail since then. How does it work?

REAL ESTATE?

One of the most famous views in fiction must surely be Elizabeth Bennet's first sight of Pemberley in *Pride and Prejudice*:

> They gradually ascended for half a mile, and then found themselves at the top of a considerable eminence, where the wood ceased, and the eye was instantly caught by Pemberley House, situated on the opposite side of a valley, into which the road with some abruptness wound. It was a large, handsome, stone building, standing well on rising ground, and backed by a ridge of high woody hills; – and in front, a stream of some natural importance was swelled into greater, but without any artificial appearance. Its banks were neither formal, nor falsely adorned. Elizabeth was delighted.
>
> (Austen 1996: 201)

This is, of course, a critical moment in the narrative: at Pemberley, in the light of the good taste displayed in the restraint of its furnishings, and in consequence of the housekeeper's praise of its owner, Elizabeth will change her mind about Mr Darcy. And it is a critical moment in the project of the novel too: Elizabeth will acknowledge what propriety grounded in property can do, and the proprietor of Pemberley will in turn recognize the appropriateness (in every sense of that term) of a union with wit in conjunction with virtue, regardless of wealth or family. In this way, sense is allied to money by the most natural means imaginable: Elizabeth marries Mr Darcy, and the landed gentry is saved from decadence. Pemberley, as all readers can see, is a heavily moralized house: solid, sensible, not showy, and set against the landscape in a way that is consistent with nature.

What more commonly goes unsaid is that Pemberley is also visualized, rather than described. Its features are relatively few and generalized: a stone house, with a stream in front and a ridge of woods behind. But this foreground and middle ground, against a backdrop of woods, is presented to the gaze of a spectator, who looks from a specific vantage point, shared with the protagonist, apparently at the same level as the house. A 'considerable eminence' forms a natural point of view, from which 'the eye' is caught and captivated: 'Elizabeth was delighted.'

Pemberley is presented, in other words, as if it were a painting, seen from a specified position, and in perspective. When the point of view moves, the perspective alters. Inside the house, Elizabeth goes automatically to the window to examine the prospect. Now the line of sight is reversed and her previous position becomes itself a spectacle: 'The hill, crowned with wood, from which they had descended, receiving increased abruptness from the distance, was a beautiful object' (Austen 1996: 201–2). The slope they had 'gradually ascended' in the first instance is now foreshortened from Elizabeth's new location on the other side of the valley.

Again the text emphasizes what the protagonist sees, rather than simply what is there. This is as it should be, of course. The primary concerns of both the narrative and the moral theme are the perceptions of the characters: in the story the house matters because of what it tells Elizabeth. But at the same time, the account demonstrates a convergence between distinct cultural forms: narrative fiction draws on painting to tell a story that involves a building.

DESIRE AND THE VOID

Architecture, like pottery, like monumental sculpture, is a way of enclosing emptiness, marking off a space and in the first instance consecrating that (Lacan 1992: 135–6). Temples, palaces, châteaux, cathedrals and even the houses of the gentry in their own more modest way, depend for their grandeur on a size that is way in excess of anything their function requires. Magnificence may demand the intensive decoration of the building itself as the container of this emptiness, with columns and caryatids, or porticoes and pinnacles, according to style, but it also necessitates the preservation of the spaces inside that are the effect of sheer scale. To reinforce this, internal walls are pierced by arches, and ceilings vaulted or domed. Towers, turrets and spires do nothing so much as enclose absence. It its own self-deprecating way, Pemberley also lays claim to size in excess of need, though always in conjunction with elegance: 'It was a large, handsome, stone building . . . .' The dining-parlour 'was a large, well-proportioned room . . . .' 'The rooms were lofty and handsome . . . .' (Austen 1996: 201–2).

To recapitulate the argument of Chapter 5, Lacan sees the void that architecture surrounds as the place of the lost object in the inextricable real, impossible to symbolize and equally impossible to forget. The Thing, the object of the drive, constructed retroactively as forbidden, leaves a hole in what it is possible to signify, and can be represented only by emptiness. But its loss remains a source of dissatisfaction for the organism-in-culture which is the human being, and it is this structural discontent that gives rise to desire. Desire in Lacan is a desire for nothing nameable, but it finds stand-ins, often a succession of them, sutured into place as love-objects, in the course of most individual lives.

To be united with the Thing, even if it were possible, would be to surrender our existence as subjects, dissolving into pure absence. We need, therefore, to keep our distance. Architecture both invokes and circumscribes the void which is the memorial to the lost real. Enclosing emptiness, surrounding it with a substantial materiality that is shaped, styled and decorated according to taste, architecture thus reaffirms the power of culture to keep the object of the drive in its place. Much like tombs, then, but on a larger scale than most of them, grand buildings at once allude to loss and contain it, render it present and absent at the same time. They are in consequence places of desire.

Pemberley too is a place of desire. We should be wrong, I am convinced, to suppose that Elizabeth's change of heart is motivated purely by property or, indeed, by morality. The success of *Pride and Prejudice* as romantic comedy lies precisely in its power to bring together both these terms with romance, holding love, wealth and virtue together literally in one place. Elizabeth's moment of recognition is conditional precisely on Mr Darcy's absence. When they unexpectedly meet, her first feeling is one of acute embarrassment at the apparent impropriety of her presence there. As a result of their unexpected meeting in the flesh, of even this degree of proximity to the real, 'the cheeks of each', the novel records, 'were overspread with the deepest blush' (Austen 1996: 206). As so commonly in nineteenth-century fiction, the body declares what the subject is not permitted to say, but its utterance here is complex: perhaps shame, anxiety and desire in unspecified proportions.

PAINTING

It is not, then, the presence of the hero that prompts Elizabeth's conversion. Instead, the implications of her tour of Pemberley have already come together a few moments earlier, when she contemplates not his person but his picture:

> In the gallery there were many family portraits, but they could have little to fix the attention of a stranger. Elizabeth walked on in quest of the only face whose features would be known to her. At last it arrested her – and she beheld a striking resemblance of Mr Darcy, with such a smile over the face, as she remembered to have sometimes seen, when he looked at her. She stood several minutes before the picture in earnest contemplation, and returned to it again before they quitted the gallery. Mrs Reynolds informed them, that it had been taken in his father's lifetime.
>
> There was certainly at this moment, in Elizabeth's mind, a more gentle sensation towards the original, than she had ever felt in the height of their acquaintance.
>
> (Austen 1996: 205)

Elizabeth does not mistake the painting for the man. Textually, this is consistently a picture, a 'striking resemblance', with a smile on 'the face' *such as* she remembered. The portrait, rather, alludes to Mr Darcy, and by that means renders him both present and absent. His likeness resembles him (strikingly), and thus acts as a memorial to previous moments of cordiality between them, but at the same time keeps him safe in his frame, on the wall, in the gallery, half-confining the image to a specific moment now past, 'in his father's lifetime'.

What we seek in painting, Lacan affirms, is not an illusion that we are looking at the scene itself, or not *simply* an illusion. Instead, we look for an indication that the imitation of the object also declares itself to be just that, 'destroys itself, by demonstrating that it is only there as a signifier' (Lacan 1992: 136). His instance here is the Baroque style, with its elaborate play of forms, putting ornamentation on show. These glittering surfaces fence off the loss they surround, keep it at bay with a parade of pleasurable signifiers. Art, which includes architecture, of course, neither delineates the real, nor acts as a substitute for it, but alludes at the level of the signifier to the loss of the real that is the cause of discontent in the signifying subject. All art, then, is a place of desire.

We may assume that Mr Darcy's portrait owes nothing to the Baroque, and shows as much restraint as his house. Nevertheless, it is as a signifying surface that the painting arrests Elizabeth, and softens her feelings towards him.

THE ORIGINS OF PERSPECTIVE

Mr Darcy's portrait hangs in a gallery of such paintings. If the outsides of grand buildings are variously moulded and carved, the inside walls of dwellings and consecrated places, from the caves through Roman villas to medieval churches and beyond, have proved irresistible to painters. Even now, whether we cover them with frescoes, canvases, panelling, wallpaper, posters or simple household paint, we commonly decorate our walls.

At a specific historical moment, however, the imperative to make pictures of buildings promotes, Lacan says, the project of finding all over again 'the sacred emptiness of architecture in the less marked medium of painting' (1992: 136). The flat background against which medieval saints stand, as if barely detached from the walls they adorn, progressively recedes with the development of perspective, until the space behind them deepens to infinity. When the rules of perspective are invented, the three dimensions perceptible to human stereoscopic vision are reduced to two by an elaborate and historic conjuring trick, and reproduced on the single plane of a painted replica.

The reproduction of visual space did not, of course, take place overnight. In the early fourteenth century Giotto not only moulded his figures into three dimensions by his use of shadow, but also knew that parallel lines tended to converge, just as Duccio did in Siena (Kemp 1990: 9–10). In the course of the next hundred years, any number of Italian painters would gesture with increasing confidence towards the representation of depth, while in Northern Europe close attention to the effects of light on draped cloth were producing effects of three dimensions in yet other ways. But in or before 1413 Filippo Brunelleschi made a remarkable breakthrough. He apparently discovered or calculated that if all the receding lines that are understood to lie at right angles to the picture plane (the orthogonals) are brought to converge at a specific vanishing point on the horizon, and if all the objects understood to be between the picture plane and the vanishing point are diminished and foreshortened accordingly, the resulting picture will reproduce what the human eye actually perceives as a third dimension.

SPACE IN A BOX

How was this extraordinary illusion to be brought home to viewers? In the early days, when the technique was still relatively new, straight, receding lines, which met at a vanishing point, were picked out with self-conscious accuracy. In Carlo Crivelli's *Annunciation* of 1486, the wall of the Virgin's house divides the picture plane in half (Figure 6.1). The orthogonals constructed by the street and the mouldings converge perfectly on a grilled rectangle in the town wall directly below the place of God. You can test this by extending the existing lines. For instance, a ruler held against the roofline will pass through this grille, as will a similar extension of any of the lines marking off the ground floor from the floor above. The mouldings on the other side of the street can be similarly extended to lead to the identical point. Meanwhile, the Virgin inhabits a richly appointed house, with coffered ceilings that draw the eye in the same direction.

Outside in the street, St Emidius seeks permission to present the Virgin with a scale model of Ascoli, itself shown in a version of perspective. The papal bull *Libertas Ecclesiastica*, named at the bottom of the painting, had granted the town a measure of self-government on the Feast of the Annunciation four years before. The picture thus celebrates the local event at the same time as one of the most important moments in the Christian calendar, when the spirit of God makes direct contact with human flesh.

Crivelli depicts this divine emanation from the sky above the vanishing point as a line of light, which enters the Virgin's ear as the message delivered by the angel. In accordance with tradition, the

Figure 6.1 Perspective painting encloses space in a box. (Carlo Crivelli, *Annunciation*, 1486.)

Annunciation is literally an announcement, God made intelligible, presentable, at the level of the signifier. In other representations of this period, a scroll sometimes bears the words of God's greeting. The angel holds one end; the other enters the space marked off as belonging to the Virgin. Crivelli's God evidently belongs to the field of the real. The line of light that marks the flight of the Holy Ghost is depicted as perfectly straight. It ignores perspective and buildings alike, and makes a neat hole in the frieze, framed like a dove-cote, without bending to pass through it.

While the dove delivers God's message to the Virgin, the small figure of a representative of Ascoli, standing on the bridge, reads the message from the Pope, God's deputy on earth. The Pope's announcement is sent by humble carrier pigeon. The whole image appears perfectly three-dimensional to a spectator placed at a central viewpoint and with one eye closed. Even the photograph retains something of this three-dimensionality: try looking at it with one eye shut. The removal of the door to the Virgin's house, and the cessation of the paving stones at the same level, have the effect of creating a kind of stage set, or perhaps three sides of a box, within which space recedes as far as the eye can see.

BRUNELLESCHI'S CONJURING TRICK

Nature did not in the normal course of things provide straight horizontal lines at varying heights above the ground nor, indeed, floor tiles, which in instance after instance would display the geometry involved. But architecture did. Besides, Brunelleschi, constituted in the course of the fifteenth century as the founder of perspective painting, was not himself a painter but an architect, and the first recorded case of the application of the new 'science' was his small panel depicting the Baptistry of San Giovanni in Florence.

The panel has not survived, and the inaugural moment of perspective painting is now accordingly textual, rather than pictorial. It was evidently a major event. Antonio Manetti recorded what happened in the first biography of Brunelleschi, probably written in the 1480s. Manetti was born in 1423, some ten years after the episode he recounts with such conviction. If by then the occurrence has achieved a certain mythic character, that may be because all traditions have a tendency to seek a founding moment, and to invest it with decisive quality that might or might not have been apparent at the time (Damisch 1994: 75).

Within two decades of the event, this mythic status seems to have been assumed. In 1436 Leon Battista Alberti dedicated to Brunelleschi the Italian version of his treatise *On Painting*, explaining the principles of visual realism in general and perspective in particular. The invention Alberti attributes to Brunelleschi in the Dedication is the dome of Florence Cathedral, the first Renaissance dome, built between 1420 and 1436. He does not mention the perspective picture of the Baptistry. But it seems that he took Brunelleschi's role as the founder of perspective for granted, since he concludes his Dedication to him by saying, 'I want above all to be corrected by you, so as not to be criticized by detractors' (Alberti 1991: 35). This implies that Brunelleschi is the expert on perspective painting.

If his first biographer can be believed, the architect-painter knew how to put on a show. Manetti's record of Brunelleschi's first perspective painting, as befits its topic, is both detailed and specific, and enables us to imagine the event with great clarity:

> He first demonstrated his system of perspective on a small panel about half a *braccio* square [a *braccio* is just over 58 cm, so each side of the panel was probably rather less than 12 inches]. He made a picture resembling the exterior of the church of San Giovanni in Florence, representing as much of it as can be seen at a glance from the outside. In order to paint it, it seems that he stationed himself some three *braccia* inside the central portal of Santa Maria del Fiore. It was done with such care and delicacy and with such precision in the black and white colours of the marble that no miniaturist could have done it better. In the foreground he painted the part of the piazza encompassed by the eye, that is to say from the side facing the Misericordia up to the arch and corner of the sheep market, and from the side with the column of the miracle of St Zenobius up to the corner of the straw market, and as much of this place as one sees from a distance.
>
> (Manetti 1970: 42–4, translation modified)

The panel has not survived, but the buildings have. According to Manetti's account, Brunelleschi placed himself at a specific vantage point inside the Cathedral, and then reproduced with minute accuracy, including the pattern of black and white marble adorning the Baptistry, what was visible from there. This included the piazza in the foreground, and three sides of the hexagonal Baptistry, one facing him, and two receding into the distance, with as much of their surroundings as was framed by the Cathedral doorway. The vanishing point was presumably masked by the Baptistry itself, but the indications of distance beyond it, as well as the solid blocking of the building itself as a container of space, would sufficiently vindicate Lacan's point that the techniques of perspective make it possible to gesture in two dimensions to the three-dimensional emptiness which marks the absence of the lost real. If Brunelleschi's orthogonals converged, as seems likely, at the door of the Baptistry, the eye would be drawn towards the point of access to the mysterious spaces within.

THE TRUTH IN PAINTING

When it came to the sky, however, Brunelleschi encountered an element that was apparently not amenable to perspective painting. How could infinity itself, beyond the reach of the parallel lines, be captured in this geometrical mapping of space? 'How', moreover, 'is one to represent, feature by feature, a body that has no contours?' (Damisch 1994: 94). Leonardo would later recognize that strict perspective painting has trouble with nebulous forms, like water and smoke (Kemp 1990: 50). Here is Manetti's account of Brunelleschi's solution:

> And in so far as he had to show the sky, where the walls he had painted stood out against the air, he placed polished silver so that natural air and sky were reflected in it, and thus clouds were seen to be carried along in the silver when the wind blew.
>
> (Manetti 1970: 44–5)

In its inaugural moment, the new science of painting confronts one of its own limits. The actuality of the sky, in Brunelleschi's panel, was done with mirrors.

Manetti goes on to draw attention to yet another limitation intrinsic to geometrical perspective. The spectator must look from the right place, opposite the vanishing point of the picture. What is more, the full three-dimensional effect is available only to monocular vision: just as in the case of Crivelli's *Annunciation*, the objects stand out properly against the depth of field to a viewer with one eye shut. Brunelleschi's demonstration took full account of these problems. Manetti continues:

> Since in such a painting it is necessary that the painter postulate beforehand a single point from which the painting must be viewed, taking into account the length and width of the sides as well as the distance, in order that no error would be made in looking at it (since any divergence from that single point would change what appeared to the eye), he had a hole made in the painted panel at the point on the church of San Giovanni struck by the eye of anyone looking directly from the central portal of Santa Maria del Fiore for the purpose of painting it. The hole was as tiny as a lentil bean on the painted side, and on the other side it widened like a pyramid, like a woman's straw cap, to about the circumference of a ducat, or a little more. And he required anyone who wanted to look at it to place their eye on the reverse side, where the hole was large, and while bringing the hole up to the eye with one hand, to hold a flat mirror facing it with the other, so that the painting was reflected in it. The mirror was extended by the other hand a distance that more or less approximated in small *braccia* the distance in regular *braccia* from the place he appears to have been when he painted it up to the church of San Giovanni. To look at it in the specified circumstances, the polished silver, the piazza, etc., and the point, it seemed that one was seeing the truth itself. I have had it in my hands and seen it many times in my days, and can testify to it.
>
> (Manetti 1970: 44–5, translation modified)

Doing justice to Brunelleschi's little panel, then, was evidently quite a business, as perhaps befits a founding moment. Spectators who wanted to see the truth itself had to screw one eye to the back of the panel, so that they could see the image of its painted side reflected in the mirror held in their other hand, at a distance scaled for size to match the artist's original distance from the Baptistry. Only by this means could they be sure to see exactly what Brunelleschi saw and transferred to his panel, and to see it in three dimensions. And presumably, they also had to tilt the panel so that the sky was duly reflected in the polished silver.

Why this complicated procedure? To make sure, evidently, that they looked with one eye only, from exactly the right distance, directly at the vanishing point, which should ideally be level with the viewer's eye. On those conditions, and those only, the truth itself appeared in painting.

ILLUSION AND REALITY

Or rather, the truth was conjured into being. The illusion must have seemed miraculous. And the elaborate ritual with the reversed panel and the mirror could have left no doubt of the distinction between the illusion and actuality.

Meanwhile, the mirror image of the sky in the polished silver, dependent on the actual weather, but playing its part in the picture only by reflection, must have had the effect of emphasising the antithesis between the picture and the world it resembled, precisely by deconstructing the opposition between actuality on the one hand and painted image on the other. Hubert Damisch, to whose Lacanian analysis of the origins of perspective I owe much of my under-standing of this event, points out that what Brunelleschi here demonstrated, perhaps in spite of himself, was the difference between truth and reality (Damisch 1994: 139–40). Truth exists in culture, at the level of the signifier, in this instance as a painting which denotes a building. But the fact that the image is lifelike only in certain conditions of visibility, or that an instance of truth is limited by the rules that also make it possible, implies that there are more things in heaven and earth than culture can easily reproduce. The illusion must have seemed like magic, but the inclusion of the polished silver marked it *as* illusion, and inscribed in culture itself the limits to which culture is subject.

Brunelleschi continued to have trouble with the sky, which could not, strictly speaking, be included in the map of space offered by geometrical perspective, and yet was necessary to mark the horizon and thus the vanishing point of the perspective itself. Once spectators had grown accustomed to expect the illusion of space, of course, later painters could afford to be less rigid in their application of the principles. Already by the end of the century Leonardo was to recognize that where the rules conflict with plausibility, the rules must give way. Once the geometry of fixed-point monocular perspective had been internalized, it could also be ignored in a good cause (Kemp 1990: 49–50, 96–7).

But these were early days. In his second demonstration of perspective, Manetti records, Brunelleschi found another solution. This time he depicted the Piazza dei Signori and the surrounding buildings. Since this was a much bigger panel, he abandoned the procedure with the mirror as unwieldy. Apparently, the second picture was much admired: Uccello and other painters wanted to copy it. Where in the previous instance he had placed polished silver to reflect the sky, he now cut the panel along the roofline, and took it to a place where he could observe it with the natural atmosphere above the buildings (Manetti 1970: 44–7). Theoretically, at least, it must have been possible, though Manetti doesn't say so, to position yourself exactly at the correct viewpoint and, if you could get the distance right, match up the panel with its subject matter, so that the cut-out perfectly corresponded with the actual roofline, and the sky above it was the actual sky. But the condition of this remarkable display of verisimilitude would be that the image would screen out actuality itself at the level of the buildings. We should see the truth in painting, but only at the expense of the world it was true of. The imagined scene offers truth or actuality, truth and then actuality, but not both at the same time.

The signifying image, in this instance as always, supplants what it depicts. The signifier takes the place of the referent or, as Jacques Derrida would say, 'defers' it and thereby relegates it to a location from which it is not accessible as presence or idea (Derrida 1973). Brunelleschi's fretwork copy relegates the actuality of the Piazza dei Signori, however perfectly it resembles what we should see there. Indeed, the exactness of the resemblance is precisely what obscures the scene itself. A less perfect fit would no doubt allow glimpses of the actual roofline.

REALITY AND THE REAL

The Piazza, the reality we can see in the absence of its two-dimensional replica, is not the same as the real. The actuality of this square, these buildings, like Brunelleschi's picture of them, are another instance of culture, albeit in a different material. By contrast, the real, in the sense in which I am using the term, is the unknown, there, but not there-for-a-subject, and so impossible to name, depict or, indeed, build in culture.

Brunelleschi's second panel shows above all that any cultural form, however truthful, has limits, edges. It implies, therefore, that culture is always, in a sense, cut out against what necessarily exists beyond it, and constitutes its motive. But we need three distinct signifiers: culture, reality and the real. Beyond the (cultural) panel lies (cultural) reality, the Piazza, rendered invisible by the panel; but beyond culture in its entirety there resides what cannot be seen from within it. Culture itself is another kind of fretwork, a cut-out that screens the real, while at the same time encircling the vacancy that alludes to its loss.

THE TRIUMPH OF PERSPECTIVE

Undaunted by the limitations of the form, or challenged, indeed, to overcome them, perspective painting, as we know, went from strength to strength. It defined the Italian Renaissance. In the Netherlands a whole seventeenth-century school would be devoted to depicting the consecrated emptiness of churches, often breaking with geometry and enlarging the space of the vault, in the interests of preserving the vertical lines of the side walls and the pillars.

Another Dutch school, roughly contemporary with it, would specialize in domestic interiors, mapping the effects of light admitted by the large glass windows now cheaply available to the middle class, the door frames cutting off our access to the rooms they also imply. Even domesticity has its mysteries, its private places. Indeed, in the 1650s Samuel van Hoogstraten put a whole house in a little box, and invited viewers to explore, through a peephole in each side, much in the manner of Brunelleschi's first panel, the passages giving onto invisible spaces, which seem miraculously to recede beyond the capacity of the box itself. The box, with its peephole and its magic mirrors, is on display in the National Gallery, London.

Italian Renaissance architecture-as-painting within architecture caused painted illusionistic spaces to open up inside existing rooms, and Baroque ceilings to soar away into the Empyrean. If the strict rule by which the eye of the viewer must be matched up with the vanishing point has softened by this time, the image is still delivered to a specific point of view, imposing limits on the position from which the illusion makes sense. In due course, the three-dimensionality of Canaletto's eighteenth-century cityscapes would depend on the orthogonals created by the line of the buildings and their reflections on water, the point of view often magically floating unsupported in mid air (Figure 6.2).

TIME AND PLACE

Evidently, Brunelleschi's successors did not share his anxieties about the sky. But there was a price to pay for specifying the weather, however serene. The polished silver of the San Giovanni panel preserved the image in a timeless present: this moment's weather provided the backdrop for the enduring Baptistry. By this ingenious means, therefore, Brunelleschi effectively conquered time as well as space, and the Baptistry's emptiness was invested by art with a kind of permanence. Come rain or shine, the panel would continue to stand as testimony to architecture's power to contain absence.

In this respect, Brunelleschi sustained something of the late medieval tradition, where saints stand in their niches for ever against the gold of heaven, or the events of the Old Testament and the New take place simultaneously. An *Annunciation* of the early 1430s (now in the Prado, Madrid), still sustains it twenty years after Brunelleschi's invention. There Fra Angelico shows the hem of Gabriel's garment and the tips of his wings projecting into the space where another angel in matching uniform drives Adam and Eve out of Paradise. The Incarnation will reverse the effects of the Fall, and the meaning of the Christian story is rendered timeless by the continuity within a single image of the salvation promised by the Annunciation and the Expulsion of Adam and Eve from the Garden of Eden as a

Figure 6.2 The space Canaletto depicts is confined to a single moment. (Canaletto, *The Upper Reaches of the Grand Canal*, about 1738.)

punishment for their sin. Crivelli's *Annunciation* exploits the convention in a different way: the Church calendar, annually re-enacting
biblical events, permits the arrival of the divine and papal messages
to coincide.

But the new science of perspective, committed to another kind of
truth in painting, a fidelity to what the eye actually sees, came in
due course to acknowledge the necessity of specifying the time and
place of the act of seeing. In a scene by Canaletto, for example, it
would generally be possible to construe not only the season of year,
but also the time of day. More important (since in a sense we also
know the time of year of the Annunciation), Canaletto depicts the
sky as it could be seen at one unique (if probably imaginary) instant.

Perspective thus narrows the possibilities in yet another respect.
The image is increasingly expected to settle for a single tense and a
single location. If the Annunciation is a unique historical event, its
meaning is endlessly repeated, nevertheless, we are to understand,
both in the festivals of the Church and the lives of countless individuals. The picture that emphasizes its meaning therefore has no
specific tense, but is capable of spanning past, present and future.
Fra Angelico achieves this by ignoring photographic realism, or the
construction of the illusion that the spectator is looking at an actual
event. Instead, he shows the Fall and the Annunciation taking place
at the same time and in the same space. Crivelli transcends the limitations of his own perspective in the straight line marking the flight
of the Holy Ghost as unconstrained by human concepts of space, as
well as by the ingenuity of bringing together the divine message
with the papal announcement on the Feast Day of the Annunciation.
But even if the Grand Canal looks much the same day after day,
Canaletto, strictly speaking, catches the sky at a unique moment.
And equally strictly speaking, he shows these boatmen doing these
things at a specific instant, just as if the camera had caught them in
a snapshot.

Culture's miracle, constructing the three-dimensional space of
desire out of flat picture plane and paint, is achieved at a considerable price. Faithful to a specific actuality, illusionism puts on display
a moment the painter chooses, investing the artist with autonomy,
or with perfect sovereignty over the material we see. But for the

viewer, this moment is always elsewhere, unattainable, lost. I can visit Venice now, and see the Grand Canal with many of its buildings in place. It is not quite clear how I could stand unsupported in the position from which I would view Canaletto's scene. But above all, I can never recover the exact instant the artist depicted.

As it pacifies the drive, fencing off the pure absence of the Thing, perspective painting opens a space of loss that perpetuates the desire of the viewer.

7

DESIRE AND THE MISSING VIEWER

ANNIHILATION

Perspective gives, then, and it takes away. It gives the miracle of a simulated reality so palpable that we might be there, and in the process installs us as viewing subjects, sovereign over all we survey. At the same time, perspective narrows that reality to a moment already lost (or, just possibly, in the future), so that, conversely, we cannot be there. Is there thus a sense in which it also takes us away, subtracts the viewer from the viewing process?

The Cartesian I *think*, as origin, presses towards idealism. Why should not Descartes's *cogito*, taken to its logical conclusion, go so far as to endow the subject with the dizzying capacity to annihilate what it sees? This, Lacan points out, was Berkeley's question. How, Berkeley wondered, do I know that the world is still there when I am not looking at it? It is as if my representations *belong to me*, and I take them with me when I leave. 'This', Lacan comments, 'is how the world is struck with a presumption of idealization, of the suspicion of yielding me only my representations' (1979: 81).

How comfortable such an idealist world would be, giving me back only what I put there − and, at the same time, how dull, how impoverished. I should wander alone through a fictitious universe of my own making. There would be nothing to know, nothing to want to know, since I could make up any answer I chose. There would be nothing to discuss – and no one, of course, to discuss it with, since any other people there were would be living their own fantasies. If I existed at all in these, I should do so purely as they represented me, with no possibility of resisting their representations. Berkeley did not believe it, of course, and invoked God to keep an eye on things, making sure they were still there when he himself turned his back.

Without God, or without the real, there is nothing obvious to counter the idea that what we see belongs to us, and that we are therefore able to annihilate it. In this view, the interpretation of art belongs entirely to the viewer: a world without alterity allows paintings no independent existence. The culturalist position attributes a similar power to culture, rather than the individual. Culture, which makes us what we are, defines what we see.

But what if the positions were reversed? What if, in other words, the picture takes upon itself the idealist position, and calls into question the existence of the viewer? Is it possible? What would it mean? Would it matter?

THE GAZE

That other people see us goes some way to reassure us that we exist. They don't see the whole truth about us, of course, for better or worse. But we are visible – shopping, making notes, walking to work. Psychoanalysis takes account of this elementary reassurance in the scopic field. Just as the condition of speaking was the prior existence of a language to speak in, looking is possible on the basis of a prior state of seeing: we see and are seen reciprocally. A single cultural gesture produces the domain of the visible and my capacity to look. By this means we begin to be caught in the butterfly net of culture itself. (Visually impaired people also imagine spatial relations; meanwhile, some of their corresponding reassurance also comes from the sound of voices, which they often hear more acutely than fully sighted people.)

Freud maintains that the scopic drive begins as narcissism. The child looks at part of its own body. Later, there develops a split within this gratifying unity: the subject looks at what are now identifiably other people; other people look at the child. The process of looking becomes reversible, and the once undifferentiated gaze is now divided between seeing and being seen (1984: 127).

That split, the loss of the unified gaze, when looking and being looked at occur at once, and from the same place, constitutes, Lacan argues, the object-cause of desire in the field of the visible. Mirrors reproduce some of the primary narcisissism, allowing me the partial illusion that I see myself from the place where I am also seen. But pictures belong to the symbolic, defined by the incursion of difference. The most gratifying – and quite impossible – picture would return our look, but submissively, seeing us as we want to be seen. (Much photographic pornography simulates an element of this: the model gazes invitingly back at the viewer, offering to belong to him in fantasy.)

Conversely, the missed gaze elicits desire. Is there something in this? Isn't Leonardo's *Mona Lisa* the best-known painting ever? This image in the Louvre has fascinated generations of tourists from all over the world. Why? Among other reasons, because, surely, she *almost* meets our gaze. 'Her eyes follow you round the room', people say. They do, but they look very marginally to one side of ours, wherever we stand. Moreover, they look without seeing, or without seeing the viewer. Like Titian's desiring Venuses, Mona Lisa stares into a mysterious distance, as if seeking the object-cause of her own desire. The extraordinary capacity of oil paint to produce the illusion of flesh creates a figure who seems palpable, and yet does not acknowledge the look she (almost) meets. Instead, she replicates the action of the viewer, who looks at her, or perhaps somewhere beyond her, into the fantastic depths of the painting.

In the missed encounter between gazes, Lacan would identify the *objet a*, the object that comes to replace the Thing in his account, as the void that meets unconscious desire, in consequence of its alienation in the symbolic. Mona Lisa's gaze seduces and teases, at once promising and withholding a place of recognition for the spectator.

THE ARNOLFINI BETROTHAL PORTRAIT

In practice, all pictures are necessarily 'blind' in this way, luring the viewer into a place of desire. But some do so more explicitly than others. Jan van Eyck's double portrait of Giovanni Arnolfini and Jeanne Cenami offers to incorporate the place of the viewer, and then fills the space with two other figures who belong to its own vanished moment. It thus does away, in effect, with the spectator to whom the couple are so evidently presented.

Just over two decades after Brunelleschi's remarkable discovery, though with no means of knowing it had taken place, Van Eyck arrived by independent means at something very similar to fixed-point perspective. In the Arnolfini portrait the orthogonals do not quite converge on a single vanishing point, though the composition lines have the effect of leading the eye to the gleaming mirror on the back wall (Figure 7.1). This painting implies that the floorboards continue in front of the picture plane, permitting the illusion that we share the same domestic space as the couple. The verisimilitude in the rendering of light on surfaces – fabric, metal, boards – is remarkable.

Van Eyck's portrait evidently celebrates the betrothal of the merchant and his prospective bride in 1434 (Hall 1994). Giovanni Arnolfini is depicted in the act of taking an oath, his right hand raised, just as in modern American courts of law. The linked hands of the couple show the nature of the promise. In addition, the bed so clearly indicated behind Jeanne Cenami (her garment touches it), while displaying the wealth and status of the couple, also specifies the sexual meaning of the conjugal relation. Two witnesses appear as tiny figures in the convex mirror beyond their reflected backs, and Van Eyck's formal signature on the wall above it guarantees not only the attribution of the picture, but the artist's presence at the ceremony: 'Johannes de eyck fuit hic [Jan van Eyck was here] 1434.' The portrait evidently focuses on the contract between the couple, even if it does not constitute the 'marriage certificate' Erwin Panofsky believed it to be (Panofsky 1953: 201–3).

Does the Arnolfini panel depict desire in the Lacanian sense? Not at first glance, perhaps. The distance between the figures, his hand supporting but not clasping hers, not to mention the voluminous

Figure 7.1 Van Eyck's mirror banishes the viewer. (Jan van Eyck, *The Arnolfini Double Portrait*, 1434.)

warm clothes, seem to indicate a much more formal relationship. If Jeanne stands with downcast eyes, in the manner of any nineteenth-century bride, Giovanni's expression is inscrutable: ascetic, aloof, even austere in the solemnity of the moment. And yet, perhaps we can detect a trace of desire precisely in what is not said, in the disjunction between the intimacy implied by the outdoor pattens kicked off in this private setting, the presence of the bed and the unreadable expressions of the couple, who do not quite look at one another. Is there here a beginning of the construction of a desiring interiority, an inward place of lack inaccessible to the viewer and possibly even to the figures themselves?

However that may be, Van Eyck has brilliantly solved one of the problems of perspective painting, its confinement to what can be seen from a specified point of view. The mirror behind the couple permits vision through 360 degrees, its convex surface reflecting the room back to us in detail from the opposite side, including the bench under the window and the shutter obscured by Giovanni, as well as the second window that illuminates Jeanne, creating the deep shadows in the folds of her train that are among the main sources of verisimilitude.

But once again there is a price to pay for overcoming a limitation. As viewers of the scene, we should be visible between the witnesses and the couple, or where the witnesses stand, on the assumption that one of them is the artist, since our view of the room is unimpeded. The mirror, however, by showing the whole space, makes clear that we are not there, renders us invisible, withholds the reassuring gaze. The completeness of the image has the explicit effect of eliding the body of the spectator.

But of course we are not there! The time of the painting is specified in the inscription. It is 1434. And the tense is indicated too. Jan van Eyck 'fuit hic', *was* here. This is the perfect tense of a completed action, the historic past, the tense of narrative (compare Jane Austen's narrative tense: 'Elizabeth was delighted').

The desire depicted or, rather, not depicted, in the Arnolfini portrait thus attains a peculiar status. It is present in front of us, to the degree that we are provided with our viewpoint by the near-perspective techniques of making space, and are invited to imagine that we stand on the same floorboards as the couple and could touch the fabric of their clothes. But at the same time it is also absent, in so far as we experience these illusions in relation to an event that proclaims itself over and done with. Van Eyck, we are to understand, saw this scene and reproduced it in paint, including the reflection of himself seeing it. And his declaration marks its completion: 'Jan van Eyck was here.' By its realism, the painting shares in what Roland Barthes describes as 'that rather terrible thing which is there in every photograph: the return of the dead' (Barthes 1982: 9). In consequence, the picture itself invites our desire, by at once alluding to and burying the element of the real that is enlisted in the sexual relation. Scene of a presence and an absence, the space created by the painting becomes itself a place of desire for the spectator.

Perspective plays a specific part in this process. On the one hand, perspective painting has the effect of effacing the picture plane itself and the surface of the paint that constructs the illusion. We are encouraged to feel as if we are there, seeing what the artist saw. In his handbook on verisimilitude for painters, Alberti insisted that, as a painter himself, he began by drawing a rectangle, 'which I regard as an open window through which the subject to be painted is seen' (Alberti 1991: 54). Leonardo claimed a picture was like an object viewed through transparent glass (Damisch 1994: 239). The spectator, then, represents the fourth wall of the three-sided box of space that is a perspective picture. But, on the other hand, the pictorial surface also exists as an obstacle to our entering into the box, or, conversely, to any intrusion from it into the viewer's world of the marks of the exiled real. So in this sense the paint itself constitutes the fourth wall.

The pictorial surface makes clear that a painting is no more than a painting, proclaims it a signifier. In the case of the Arnolfini portrait, while the brush strokes efface themselves and simulate textures, the surface of the painted oak panel is nevertheless the place of Van Eyck's inscription and the perfect tense that keeps desire in its place. That place is the space of the painting.

In addition, however, in this instance the portrait teases the viewer with a promise of narcissistic gratification that it also withholds. Its indifference to us invites a certain unconscious envy, though this is by no means envy of the couple themselves, the figures in the painting. Lacan draws attention to the fact that in its Latin form, invidia, envy comes from videre, to see. And his paradigm case is the child St Augustine describes, pale with envy as he sees his foster-brother at the breast (1979: 115–16; cf. 1977: 20). Envy, Lacan insists, is not to be confused with jealousy: what we envy is not necessarily what we want. The envious child in Augustine's account is fully fed (Augustine 1912: 19–20).

What, then, makes him pale? 'The image of a completeness closed upon itself', Lacan replies (1979: 116). The mirror in Van Eyck's portrait offers us vision through 360 degrees. We should be at the centre of this space. Instead, the painting depicts a completeness closed upon itself, where we have no place.

DESIRE

None of this, Lacan insists, is necessarily evident at a conscious level. The knowing subject knows perfectly well that the painting is no more than representation (1979: 106). But the Arnolfini portrait is widely admired: something draws people to look repeatedly at a painting of a long-dead couple, who manifest no particular beauty.

Perspective painting evokes emotion not simply by its subject matter, and not only by offering a place of imaginary mastery for the spectator. In addition, it excites unconscious desire. First, in offering real-ism, it paradoxically veils the real, like Brunelleschi's fretwork panel. Second, in so far as it portrays an event, perspective sets this elsewhere, while at the same time making its moment pass for, but not supplant, the present. Third, by at once denying and insisting on the pictorial surface, it tantalizes us with the promise of direct access to a world beyond words, only to reaffirm that the source of that access is itself a signifying image, and the effect of an artistic discipline at least as complex of the rules of language. And finally, perspective restricts what can be seen to a specified angle, so that some part of the space it defines is always concealed, excluded or obscured.

By expanding the spectator's limited point of view with a mirror, however, the Arnolfini portrait also explicitly deletes the physical presence of the viewer from the scene depicted. Rather than the desolate sovereignty available to the subject of idealism, this portrait offers the viewer a measure of unconscious desire. The marks of the exiled real are the occlusions and concealments, the elisions, including the past tense and the pictorial surface, which function like discreet 'no entry' signs at an opening that at once promises and bars access.

In place of the lost real, the picture enlists the viewer in a search for the symbol of its loss, the gaze as elusive *objet a* that would, if it could, bring us into the space of the visible. No such object can be found. Instead, the point that draws the eye, the mirror on the back wall, shows the couple with their backs to us, banishing us, annihilating an existence of which they can have no knowledge and with which they self-evidently have no concern.

THE INVISIBLE ARTIST

Our surrogate does appear in the mirror, however. The tiny figures of two witnesses are just detectable there, one of them presumably the artist, who lays such prominent textual claim to have been present. In perspective painting, the viewer looks from the place of the artist, sees what the artist sees. This acts as a guarantee of the 'truth' of the image and helps to allay the anxiety of our disappearance by installing us in a privileged place, restoring the pleasure unconscious envy threatened to subtract.

A book illustration demonstrates this principle. In Chapter 8 of Charles Dickens's *Bleak House* Esther Summerson and Ada Clare reluctantly follow Mrs Pardiggle into the ground-floor room of a brickmaker's cottage. Esther describes the scene in the first person:

> Besides ourselves, there were in this damp offensive room – a woman with a black eye, nursing a poor little gasping baby by the fire; a man, all stained with clay and mud, and looking very dissipated, lying at full length on the ground, smoking a pipe; a powerful young man, fastening a collar on a dog; and a bold girl, doing some kind of washing in very dirty water. They all looked up at us as we came in, and the woman seemed to turn her face towards the fire, as if to hide her bruised eye; nobody gave us any welcome.
>
> (Dickens 1996: 130)

The ensuing failure of Mrs Pardiggle to communicate with a single member of this audience, to whom she reads aloud from an improving book, is the object of Dickens's satire here on middle-class benevolence.

Esther's verbal 'picture' lays out for us what she sees from a position evidently just inside the door: the inhabitants look up as the party comes in. The fireplace must be on another wall, since the woman turns away from them towards it; the positions of the other figures are not specified. We stand where Esther stands.

The first edition of the novel was illustrated by Hablôt K. Browne, or 'Phiz'. Phiz's drawing of this scene shows the figures, exactly as Esther has described them, distributed in plausible positions; it also shows Esther and Ada just inside the door looking at them, along with the appalling Mrs Pardiggle and her five children, and two additional figures behind them, 'friends of the young man whom we had attracted to the doorway' (130) (Figure 7.2). Phiz has thus

Figure 7.2 In this illustration of *Bleak House* we see the 'author' who describes the scene (Esther), but not the artist who draws it. (Phiz, *The visit at the Brickmaker's*, 1853.)

changed the reader's point of view, so that we also see Esther, the textual 'artist' who depicted the scene for us in the novel. Instead of imagining the episode, as the narrative invites us to, from Esther's position, we now see it from a third place, on the other side of the room. The scene is still laid out for us, on condition that we change our angle on it.

Of course, this is perfectly legitimate: part of the comedy of the ensuing scene depends on the overcrowding caused by Mrs Pardiggle's charitable visit, and to do justice to that, the image has to include all the people present. Moreover, the novel itself often looks over Esther's shoulder as she writes, its ironies inviting the reader to see beyond the limitations of her perspective.

It is also perfectly conventional. What we do not see in Phiz's illustration from our new point of view is Phiz himself. Of course not. The viewer now looks from the place, scaled to size, of the visual artist, and once again sees what the artist depicts. There is no mirror in this drawing – and no motive for a mirror. The point of view of the spectator of a perspective image, prescribed by Brunelleschi's experiment and Albertian theory, is consistently synonymous with the point of view of the painter, even when both scene and point of view are themselves fictitious. Here, as in most perspective pictures, the place of the spectator is privileged. Invisible as we are, we share, none the less, the 'original' vision of the artist.

LAS MENINAS

But there are exceptions. What happens to the viewer when the place of the artist is called into question?

As the King's Chamberlain, and thus keeper of the royal paintings at the court of King Philip IV, Diego Velázquez would have known the Arnolfini portrait, which was in the Spanish royal collection in 1656 when he painted *Las Meninas* (Figure 7.3). Velázquez was fascinated by mirrors, and owned ten of them himself (Kemp 1990: 105).

The first impression of this painting must surely be that it represents reality itself. Thanks to the first biography of the artist, written by Antonio Palomino in 1724, all the figures but two can be named. Moreover, subsequent research has not only confirmed

Figure 7.3 Where is Velázquez standing when he paints *Las Meninas?*
(Diego Velázquez, *Las Meninas*, 1656.)

the historical existence of these individuals, and the precise room
in the former Alcázar palace where the picture was painted, but has
also identified the works of art on the back wall. The five-year-old
Infanta Margarita, Palomino reveals, is accompanied by the aristocratic maids of honour of the title, as well as Mari-Bárbola, and a
mastiff so disciplined that it remains impassive even when kicked
by Nicolas Pertusato, maintained at court, like Mari-Bárbola, for his

diminutive stature (1987: 164–5). Reflected in the mirror on the back wall, differentiated from the surrounding pictures by its bevelled edge and a greyish-blue sheen, are King Philip and his second wife, Mariana.

The King, Palomino says, treated Velázquez as a friend and confidant, and often looked in to watch him work. Philip had good reason to be impressed by the painter's fidelity to the truth in painting. On one occasion he spoke to a portrait that was half-concealed in the shadows: 'What? Are you still here? Have I not already dismissed you?' (Palomino 1987: 152). He frequently turned up to watch the artist painting *Las Meninas*, as did the Queen, the Infantas and their ladies, 'considering this a delightful treat and entertainment' (166). The picture, then, portrays one of these informal gatherings, brilliantly but also deferentially breaking with the formalities of stiff royal portraiture, and Velázquez tactfully but decisively lays claim to a certain standing as court artist, by including himself at work in his own painting.

Nineteenth-century critics were so dazzled by the realism of the depiction, and the way it catches the figures as if by surprise, that they compared it to a photograph (Justi 1889: 419). It is hard not to sympathize with the German art historian, Karl Justi, when he claimed that the painting seems positively to offer access to time travel:

> The golden frame becomes a setting for a magic mirror which annihilates the centuries, a telescope for distance in time, revealing the spectral movements of the inmates of the old palace over two hundred years ago. In this picture the ideal of the historian has become truth and reality.
>
> (420)

So much truth seems to call for a narrative. Justi's account has the royal couple providing a sitting for their portrait, and sending for the Infanta as light relief. The King saw here the opportunity for another painting, and Velázquez began on it at once. So, paradoxically, this is a picture of the production of a picture (416–18).

If this nineteenth-century story seems quaint now, it is worth bearing in mind that Jonathan Brown, the modern art historian who has done much to inspire recent attention to *Las Meninas*, also sees it as capturing a moment. In his first account he argued that the Infanta had come to see Velázquez at work and had asked for a drink of water. At that moment the royal couple arrived, and the group are represented in various stages of awareness of their presence (Brown 1978: 91). More recently, Brown has been persuaded that the mastiff is one of the King's hunting dogs, and that Nicolas Pertusato is nudging it awake, so that the royal couple can leave through the door opened at the back by José Nieto, the Queen's Chamberlain (Brown and Garrido 1998: 184).

FOUCAULT'S READING

The other major influence on recent thinking about the picture has been Michel Foucault, who approaches it from a rather different angle. The Infanta's gaze, Foucault points out, is intelligible as directed to the place where the royal couple must be standing, if their images are to be reflected in the mirror in the centre of the back wall. But so too is the painter's. If the source of natural light that makes the foreground visible occupies virtually the whole of the right-hand edge of the painting, most of the left-hand side is filled by the dark back of the canvas, and this is enigmatic to us as viewers because we cannot see what it depicts. The painter, poised to add to his own canvas, studies his subject intently, and this subject is the royal couple.

The actual topic of this painting, the sovereign power which presumably commands it, and which the gaze of the painter and the Infanta acknowledge, is thus both present and absent: present as reflected in the mirror, but absent from the scene we are looking at, precisely in the sense that what we perceive of it is no more than a reflection. We cannot, in other words, see the King and Queen themselves. In this respect, Foucault proposes, what the picture is 'about' is representation itself in what he calls the 'Classical' period. And this representation is paradoxically empty. Invoking all the resources of fixed-point perspective, chiaroscuro and the mirror, Velázquez produces a spectacle full of figures in a mimetic celebration of sovereignty which at the same time centres on a void. The royal couple, who are both the cause of the painting and its subject, are at once visible and invisible, paradoxically 'elided' by the very ingenuity of their depiction. Meanwhile, the painter himself, his brush suspended between the canvas and his palette, is not painting but looking, and it is on this condition that he is visible to us. The canvas itself will mask him from us the moment he returns to the activity of painting.

The canvas we *can* see thus shows an invisible picture of an absent couple by a painter who is not painting. And where, since the proud parents take our place in front of this canvas, are we, as actual spectators of the scene? Elided too, of course. Foucault puts the case that the figure in the doorway, the only person who plays no part in the proceedings, appears there as our surrogate, so that the circle of the gaze is complete. Seeing, in effect, through 360 degrees, we also see our own stand-in, a courtier who simply watches with, we might add, his hat in his hand, respectful in the presence of higher authority (Foucault 1970: 3–16).

EVENT OR PAINTING?

As a reading of the event depicted, this is surely unsurpassed – and unexpectedly Lacanian, treating power itself as an object of desire. But the paradox of Foucault's account is that, while it treats the painting as concerned with representation, it ignores its existence *as* representation. In other words, Foucault accepts the picture's own invitation to see it as an event, and not a signifier. His reading is attentive to two of the terms I have been concerned with, point of view and verisimilitude, but he ignores the pictorial surface. Once we resist the lure of illusionism, however, and attend to the surface of the work, the fourth wall that keeps us out of the event itself, it becomes evident that *Las Meninas* poses another kind of difficulty: its artist is in the wrong place.

Esther did not describe her own appearance in the brickmaker's cottage; Phiz showed her there, but was himself invisible, since his point of view was understood to be ours. The viewer of Brunelleschi's first panel would have seen an image of the Baptistry from the artist's position, and opposite, at the vanishing point, there would have been a hole the size of a lentil and perhaps, in the right light, an eye, or its pupil. When Van Eyck showed his own presence in the mirror at the event depicted in the Arnolfini portrait, he had evidently put down his paintbrush, but he was standing exactly where the artist would have to stand to see that scene in accordance with the rules of perspective painting, opposite the effective vanishing point, and thus occluding the viewer. That Van Eyck saw what we see is the guarantee of the truth of the image, even though we are not portrayed in it. But to see the scene portrayed by *Las Meninas*, Velázquez would have to stand where Foucault locates the royal couple who are the object of so many gazes. The artist would have to occupy our position, the place, scaled for size, of the spectator.

Because we can identify the room, this position can be precisely specified. There are two doors at the front, aligned with the two doors depicted at the back. The point of view is just the other side of the right-hand door, and the vanishing point that lines up with it is the open door at the back, the light framing the Queen's Chamberlain, José Nieto, whose mother's name, included, in accordance with Spanish custom, after his surname, was Velázquez (Damisch 1994: 438). The artist, the King's Chamberlain, Diego Rodriguez de Silva y Velázquez, Palomino tells us, habitually used his mother's name, in accordance with what he regards as an outlandish Andalusian custom (Palomino 1987: 140).

To see the Infanta and her retinue from the place to which the picture is addressed, the painter would have to stand symmetrically opposite his uncannily named fellow-Chamberlain, the figure Foucault identifies as the viewer's surrogate, and the only person who can see what *Las Meninas* conceals from us.

There is a possible alternative, however, and it concerns the genre of *Las Meninas*. This is in any case one of its puzzles. Is it a portrait? or a narrative painting? Or is it, instead, a self-portrait? Palomino seems to have thought so (1987: 165). (This was, after all, the age of Rembrandt.) The nineteenth-century German critic, Karl Justi, thought so too, and assumed that Velázquez, in the tradition of self-portraiture, used a mirror (Justi 1889: 418; cf. Miller 1998: 12).

But if so (and how, after all, can anyone be in two places at once, unless it's done by mirrors?), the whole painting depicts a reflection. In the absence of plate glass, it is as if a series of looking-glasses (all ten of the artist's, perhaps) were positioned along the bottom line of the canvas, standing on the floor in front of the group of figures, and the image we see is in consequence a painting of a reflection of the artist, his canvas, the Infanta, her attendants, the dog and the other mirror on the wall. On this reading, what Velázquez sees guarantees the truth of what we see, in accordance with the rules of perspective.

Once this thought has crystallized, we might begin to think of the little girl's pose as that of a child delighting in her reflection, positioning herself as the object of her own gaze, her head turned towards the right at a slight angle to the mirror, but her eyes directed squarely at the image of herself, inspecting the effect. Her free hand rests lightly on the pannier of her dress, with a view to displaying her elaborately composed sleeve to its full advantage. There would then be no division between the gazes of her attendants and the princess herself, the painter and Mari-Bárbola in the foreground: all of them are looking at the Infanta or her reflection. No wonder they appear to gaze at us, but without seeing us. No wonder their eyes, so frontal and so concentrated, seem not to engage, none the less, with the spectator's.

The painting on the canvas, the work concealed from the viewer, would then be *Las Meninas* itself, a copy of the scene the artist is studying so intently, and the work would be perfectly and brilliantly self-referential, made possible by a double relay from mirror to mirror. Moreover, the real sovereignty, on this reading, would belong not to the monarchs, but to the painter, or rather, his art.

PAINTING *OR* REALITY

It won't work. Since the door at the back constitutes the vanishing point, the mirror beside it reflects the canvas, which is roughly in the centre of a room that we see from a slight angle through the right-hand door. The King and Queen, not *Las Meninas*, are being painted here, in a picture that includes the looped crimson curtain characteristic of royal portraiture. They are also, then, presumably, the object of the painter's gaze, and there is only one mirror after all.

What are the implications of all this? The event the painting depicts is possible as an event. But its depiction is not possible in this painting, because the painter is not in the right place to paint it from. Or, to put it differently, it's possible as a painting, on condition that it's not an event, because the painter cannot paint this scene from there. What we see is not what the artist sees. The painting triumphantly imagines an impossible set of spatial relations, and convinces us that we have seen that.

As, of course, we have, on condition that what the painting shows is not its own moment, but history. Such an event could have taken place, and Velázquez may well have recreated it here. But if so, the tense is not that of the Arnolfini portrait, where the perfect tense of the signature on the pictorial surface refers to the moment in the past when the painter stood opposite the scene he depicted with such fidelity that he showed his own reflection in the mirror on the back wall. Van Eyck's past tense refers back to the present of the act of painting.

By contrast *Las Meninas* shows a remembered moment which is not the time of its own painting, but instead a pluperfect event which *had* happened at some time before the picture was painted. A moment, in other words, which was already lost.

DESIRE AND THE ABSENT VIEWER

Reality resides in the figures whose expressions and poses are so lifelike that they could have been caught in a snapshot. Meanwhile, allusion to the lost real in *Las Meninas* is where Lacan would have located it: in the vast, shadowy spaces of the cavernous room in the royal palace, and in the turned canvas, which withholds its secret, while permitting us a blurred glimpse of its painted side in the mirror. And it is also there in the pluperfect tense of a lost past unable to be recovered, though a signifying pictorial surface can memorialize it brilliantly.

Tantalized by the image, subsequent artists, most notably Picasso, have been drawn to produce their own versions. This iconic cultural object is thrilling precisely as a painting, as a signifier, for ever divorced from the real. While art historians have searched the archive for information that would restore the truth of the story it seems to tell, viewers are lured into its depth of field in the hope of finding the *objet a*, the return of the gaze that would restore an undifferentiated looking. Unable to share the vision of the artist, who is in the wrong place to paint the scene, we find as his surrogate the relatively insignificant figure of the other Velázquez, the Chamberlain in the doorway. But he sees what we do not; we cannot see what he sees, which might or might not be the secret of the painting.

The pictorial surface of *Las Meninas* offers visual pleasure in abundance, while the impossible place of the viewer motivates the scopic drive, and promises a satisfaction it continues to withhold. The fascination of the picture depends on the fact that what it represents is not at my disposal. The representation it constitutes does not belong to me, withholds the sad, narcissistic gratification of idealism, and insists on its own irretrievable alterity.

Or, to put the issue in less individualistic terms, something in this painting continues to elude the cultural script. That something is what makes *Las Meninas* an object of desire.

8

THE REAL AND THE SUBLIME

Kant, Lyotard, Lacan

THE POSTMODERN SUBLIME

Perhaps as a way of naming the element of unconscious desire involved in our relation to cultural texts, the sublime, dear to the hearts of Romantic poets and painters, has undergone a major revival in recent years. Transcending the everyday, the Romantic sublime was a way of naming whatever seemed to soar above the reach of Enlightenment rationality. In the 1990s, however, it took on less positive connotations as a sense of the inadequacy of human experience in the face of the absolute. Both versions are traceable to Immanuel Kant, who addressed the question in the *Critique of the Power of Judgment*. In Kant's account, imagination recoils when confronted by grandeur, until thought grasps the absolute as idea, and rejoices in its own capacity to apprehend the infinite. Now prominent in the work of thinkers as influential and as relatively diverse as Jean-François Lyotard and Slavoj Žižek, while its influence is perceptible on Roland Barthes and Gilles Deleuze, the sublime has become postmodern.

But does the term illuminate our own cultural moment as much as we like to believe? Does it genuinely permit us to think more clearly about the postmodern condition? My own view is that in the end the sublime retains too much from its Romantic moment, carries too much theology in secular guise, to clarify areas of culture where clarity is most needed. Despite its creative appropriation to challenging – and quite different – effect by both Lyotard and Žižek, the attribution of sublimity always seems to entail a value judgement, for better or worse. By tracing the intertextual descent of the sublime from its earlier development in Kantian aesthetics, we can perhaps identify more sharply what the current use of the term in cultural criticism both reveals and obscures.

KANTIAN AESTHETICS

As I see it, the interest in the sublime arises in the first instance from the fact that, until quite recently, cultural criticism has lacked a theory of its own. After insisting on the empirical for so long, the critical discussion of art history, literature and popular culture first turned for theoretical analysis of its own project to the only place where theory was then to be found. That was philosophy. But philosophers have traditionally been more concerned with what it would be right to think than with what people have actually thought, and not much interested, therefore, in the way culture works. Largely indifferent, in other words, to the possibilities of cultural criticism as an account of social values, philosophers interested in culture have traditionally focused their attention on what can be thought to *have* value as art, constructing the category of aesthetics as a framework for their assessments.

Aesthetics, in turn, always leads back to Immanuel Kant, whose third *Critique* sets up a binary opposition between the beautiful and the sublime, in which the beautiful is seen as pleasurable and satisfying, while the sublime is wild, paradoxical and thrilling. According to Kant, the pleasure of the beautiful is positive; it assumes a perfection of form. The sublime, however, represents a negative kind of pleasure, because no form can do it justice. But the sublime pleasure is all the more intense for that. The inability to grasp or make present the absolute initially produces a 'momentary inhibition of the vital powers', but when reason makes possible the comprehension of the infinite, this is immediately followed by an 'all the more powerful outpouring of them' (Kant 2000: 129). The metaphor makes very clear which of these terms is sexier (cf. Derrida 1987b: 103).

THE LEGACY OF KANT

The sexiness was certainly obvious to Roland Barthes, when he set up in *The Pleasure of the Text* his own binary opposition between the text of pleasure and the text of bliss. On the one hand, the text of pleasure 'contents, fills, grants euphoria'. This is 'the text that comes from culture and does not break with it', which is consequently 'linked to a *comfortable* practice of reading'. On the other hand, the text of 'bliss' (*jouissance*) 'imposes a state of loss' and 'brings to a crisis' the reader's 'relation with language' (Barthes 1976: 14). In Kant the mind, confronted by infinity, by a grand and uncultivated landscape, or by the immeasurable scale of the Milky Way, at first retreats before the impossible effort of making present to the imagination the limitlessness they suggest. The absolute cannot take shape or form; it exists only in our ideas. Meanwhile, in Barthes's rereading of Kant, textual *jouissance* is just as ineffable. 'Pleasure can be expressed in words', Barthes claims, but 'bliss cannot' (21).

The distinction he makes here between two kinds of texts rewrites his own earlier contrast between the readable (*lisible*) text we 'consume' and the writable (*scriptible*) text, which we could not find in any bookshop (Barthes 1975: 4–6). Here too we may recognize a line of descent. In Kant's account, the inability to make present the absolute prompts reason to act where imagination fails. The sublime awakens 'the feeling of a supersensible faculty in us' (Kant 2000: 134). It affirms the capacity of the subject to overcome the limitations imposed by our senses: 'That is sublime which even to be able to think of demonstrates a faculty of the mind that surpasses every measure of the senses' (134).

What cannot be made present objectively can, in other words, be thought subjectively (151). If in the late twentieth century Roland Barthes was somewhat less optimistic about the capabilities of the subject than the Enlightenment philosopher who was to become a hero of Romanticism, he perceived the writable text, nonetheless, as an affirmation of '*ourselves writing*', in defiance of the limitations imposed by culture. It represents the creation of a self 'before the infinite play of the world . . . is traversed, intersected, stopped, plasticized by some singular system (Ideology, Genus, Criticism)' (Barthes 1975: 5).

To the degree that cultural phenomena are divided according to criteria traceable in the end to the distinction between the beautiful and the sublime, it is immediately apparent which of these is more likely to excite us now. The influence of Kantian aesthetics is frequently to be found wherever a value judgement is formulated or a preference defended, and in particular wherever modernism is contrasted with mimetic art forms. Barthes's writable text represents an ideal. The sublime, meanwhile, explicitly underwrites Gilles Deleuze's argument that the 'great' writers 'push language as a whole to its limit, to its outside, to its silence' (1998: 113). It overtly provides the framework for Jean-François Lyotard's distinction between conventional realism and the challenge of the avant-garde (1984: 71–82).[1] Yet in the process – and this is the source of my anxiety here – invocation of the sublime tends to take us, however sceptical the intention, back to the Romantic secularization of religion. It thus leads, willy-nilly, into a realm of mystery, metaphysics, transcendence or horror, a secular heaven or hell inhabited by the ghost of theology. And from the transcendence of this realm, critics commonly exercise a quasi-divine power of judgement.

Of course, the postmodern invocation of the sublime tends to stress the first half of Kant's account, the inability of the imagination to present the absolute. It generally places a question mark over the second half, its corollary, the ability to think the supersensible, which is for Kant the cause of our delight in the sublime. But reversing the values of an analysis leaves the framework itself in place and in the French appropriation of Kant the absolute commonly takes on the status of art's unattainable object of desire.

VALUE JUDGEMENTS

By this means, aesthetics imports into the analysis of culture the project of establishing criteria for value judgements that my own preferred more anthropological approach to cultural criticism finds irrelevant. We do not generally ask of tribal cultures whether their beads are better or worse than their baskets, since, however imperialist the overall ethnographic project may have come to seem, our interest has been in understanding the relations between the different practices of other cultures, not in privileging one practice over another. But in discussions of our own culture, judgements of value are never, it seems, very far away. There is nothing wrong, of course, with having – and defending – preferences, but that process is no substitute for interpretation of the meanings inscribed in cultural artefacts, however humble some of these may be.

The Romantic elevation of the sublime inherits a long Western association between art and theology. Visual art, in particular, sustains into our own period the mystical aloofness and spiritual value conferred by its pedagogic role in medieval and Renaissance Christianity. This supernatural aura, secularized but not eliminated by Romanticism, is sustained in the current resemblance between art galleries and temples. Tate Modern, for example, promisingly appropriated a former London power station as its new home, but succeeded in bringing out the industrial building's resemblance to a cathedral in the process.

So deep is the imbrication of art and religion in our culture that we readily treat cave paintings, about the origins of which we have virtually no firm information, as sacred, shamanistic symbols for our hunter-gatherer ancestors. Literary criticism in its conventional form also assumed the project of isolating the best that has been thought and said in the world. And if Cultural Studies in its early days faced an impediment to more sophisticated development, this lay above all in the resolute affirmation that popular culture was *as good as* the canonized forms. Evaluation is not the best starting point for understanding culture.

ANOTHER OPTION

Is there an alternative? In my view, if visual images and narrative fiction are to tell us anything more general about culture itself, if, in other words, we are to approach them as cultural critics rather than philosophers, we need a different vocabulary for their discussion. Ideally, such a vocabulary would be no less sophisticated and no less sympathetic than the Kantian terms, but it would permit a new take on the old questions, reformulating them in the process of reframing them. And, oddly enough, the elements of such a vocabulary show through the accounts of the postmodern sublime. They are already there for the taking.

When Terry Eagleton, for instance, sets out to read Kant's third *Critique* as a historical text in *The Ideology of the Aesthetic*, his interpretation of the sublime, paradoxically, reveals the doomed, inadequate hero of postmodern liberalism as the target of his Marxist artillery. Eagleton alludes only in passing to Kant's transcendental rescue of the rational subject, stressing instead the anguish of a solitary confrontation with the 'turbulent' experience of unaccommodated nature and the consequent collapse of metaphysical certainties. 'The subject of the sublime is . . . decentred, plunged into loss and pain', he insists (Eagleton 1990: 89). Moreover,

> It is as though in the sublime the 'real' itself – the eternal, ungraspable totality of things – inscribes itself as the cautionary limit of all mere ideology, of all complacent subject-centredness, causing us to feel the pain of incompletion and unassuaged desire.
>
> (89)

'The "real" itself.' Now, where have we come across this before? Not in Kant. Moreover, there is very little in Kant's text to justify this elegiac reading. On the contrary, for Kant the sublime affirms the capability of the thinking subject. He himself claims that the impossibility of making present the idea of the absolute shows 'our imagination in all its boundlessness, and with it nature, as paling into insignificance beside the ideas of reason' (Kant 2000, 140).

So remote is Eagleton's Kantian subject from Kant's own that we might be forgiven for assuming that this doomed, desiring creature, characterized by incompleteness, and standing on the edge of the ungraspable 'real', was familiar not so much from Kantian aesthetics, developed in the eighteenth century, as from Lacan's rereading of Freud in the twentieth.[2] And sure enough, Eagleton's chapter is headed

'The Kantian Imaginary' (70–101), invoking the term 'imaginary' in a broadly Lacanian sense. In short, Eagleton explicitly foregrounds the barely suppressed Lacanian element which in practice informs a good many versions of the postmodern sublime.

But if Lacan represents the textual intermediary between Kant and postmodernity, if Lacan's version of culture were seen to be the one at stake here after all, would it not be better to go direct to Lacan himself? If, in other words, the presence of Kantian aesthetics in cultural criticism were perceived as no more than a residue of the only official discourse available hitherto, might we not do better to look to psychoanalysis to provide an alternative terminology for cultural criticism? This would surely prove especially compelling if psychoanalysis were able to offer a vocabulary that could do without the quasi-religious connotations of the absolute, the supersensible and sublimity itself.

LYOTARD

Eagleton's immediate source here is clearly Jean-François Lyotard, the philosopher pre-eminently responsible for the wide currency of the postmodern sublime. Lyotard's Kant is more readily recognizable than Eagleton's, and the sublime is put to work in Lyotard's account in the first instance in order to specify a turning-point in cultural history.

Irritated by denunciations of the postmodern avant-garde in general, and in particular by Jürgen Habermas's argument for retaining and extending Enlightenment values, Lyotard published in Critique what the journal itself described as a combative and very personal intervention (Lyotard 1982: 357). This essay aligned the Enlightenment with realism and its false promise to tell the truth. Realism's fantasy of laying textual hands on reality itself has been, Lyotard insisted, the ally of terror – and the unspoken allusion here is to the rejection of experimental art by Nazi classicism and Stalinist Socialist Realism alike.

Modernism, by contrast, he claimed, represented the recognition that art and literature do not in practice succeed in telling it like it is. Truth cannot be made present in painting or fiction: there is always something lacking. The postmodern, which is part of the modern, he argued, rejects modernism's nostalgia for the missing truth, repudiates the consolations of good form, and celebrates instead the 'unpresentable'. Rather than conform to the existing conventions of taste, the avant-garde uncovers new rules, which become apparent only retrospectively, as the rules of *what will have been done.*

This brilliantly suggestive account, which appeared in English as 'Answering the Question: What is Postmodernism?', took the Kantian sublime as its somewhat uneasy authority for the existence of the unpresentable (Lyotard 1984: 71–82). Realism depends for its justification on the belief that the concept can be matched by an object, can, in other words, be made present to the imagination. Kant's account of the sublime showed otherwise, demonstrating, Lyotard affirms, the possibility of conceiving as an idea what exceeds the capacity of representation. As a result, 'I think in particular', he says, 'that it is in the aesthetic of the sublime that modern art (including literature) finds its impetus and the logic of the avant-gardes finds its axioms' (1984: 77).

He went on to develop this view in 'The Sublime and the Avant-Garde', where the Romantic conception of the sublime is seen as disrupting the classical, Enlightenment model of art, which depends on good taste and the presentation of shared values. The sublime, by contrast, promotes an art inspired by the unknown, which causes, in consequence, surprise, shock, pain. In its Romantic version, sublime art bears witness to the inexpressible as an idea that it struggles to represent; the modern sublime, by contrast, insists on art itself as necessarily inexpressive. Modernism does not pay tribute to a truth that resides elsewhere, but offers instead an event, an occurrence, the *something* rather than nothing, that takes place in the very process of making art happen.

This in turn paves the way, Lyotard argues, for abstraction and minimalism. 'Avant-gardism is thus present in germ in the Kantian aesthetic of the sublime' (Lyotard 1991: 98). Avant-garde art owes nothing to realism; it *tells* us nothing about the world, but instead *asks*, 'Is it happening?'. This was a question the Nazi and Stalinist regimes could not tolerate, since they wanted to be in sole control of events. They therefore deflected that issue by substituting alternative questions about the messianic future (104).

This is good and rigorous art history. My doubts about the sublime as authorizing the incommensurability of representation and the idea *now* concerns the trace of theology that survives in the investment of the unpresentable absolute with an independent existence. The Kantian heritage of the sublime implies the autonomy of the absolute. In other words, the sublime entails idealism. This is an idealism that owes as much to Plato as to German philosophy. It attributes to ideas not only primacy but, in addition, a free-standing, pre-linguistic place outside history and culture.

My unease stems partly from the view that we do not need to go back to the eighteenth century, to Kant and the sublime, to theorize the relationship between the signifier and what exceeds it. Lyotard's Kant tends to reify the unpresentable, embracing an oddly theological metaphysics. Kant, Lyotard says,

> cites the commandment, 'Thou shalt not make graven images' (Exodus), as the most sublime passage in the Bible in that it forbids all presentation of the Absolute.
>
> (1984: 78)

At the same time, however, Lyotard's Kant turns out to anticipate Lacan's distinction between the symbolic and the real. Lyotard's rereading of Kant thus bears a close resemblance to Lacan's rereading of Saussure. A return to the Saussurean and Lacanian lineage of Lyotard's Kant would have two advantages. First, Saussure's own work coincides historically with the epoch of modernism itself. And second, the Saussurean tradition makes no appeal to a metaphysics of unpresentability. Lacan's Saussure does not refer to the existence of the unpresentable in a supersensible subjective region understood as given. On the contrary, in Lacan it is the irretrievable loss of the real to the subject that makes truth problematic and realism suspect.

The religious dimension of the sublime, indicated in the vocabulary of bearing witness and the inexpressible, but otherwise kept largely at bay in the two essays I have mentioned, returns with a vengeance in Lyotard's *Postmodern Fables* ten years later. Lyotard does not, of course, affirm the supernatural, but he characterizes the absolute as the impossible object of an unattainable desire. And in the process, he makes evident the distinction he takes for granted in this context between art and the merely 'cultural'. Only a long quotation will do justice to the rhapsodic mystical and, indeed, sexual register of Lyotard's value judgement on art (eternal, aspiring) as opposed to mere culture (contingent and quotidian):

> There is no sublime object. And if there is a demand for the sublime, or the absolute, in the aesthetic sphere, it stands to be disappointed .... A sorrow felt before the inconsistency of every object, it is also the exultation of thought passing beyond the bounds of what may be presented. The 'presence' of the absolute is the utter contrary of presentation. The sign it makes escapes semiotics as it does phenomenology ....
>
> The artistic is to the cultural as the real of desire is to the imaginary of demand. The absolute is the empty name ... of that which exceeds every putting into form or object without being anywhere else but within them. The demand for forms or manners may metamorphose itself, like styles and cultures, but desire, because its object is the absolute, is unconditional. If the artfulness of great works can traverse the vicissitudes undergone by the cultural in the course of history, this is to the extent that the gesture of the work *signals* that desire is never fulfilled.
>
> (Lyotard 1997: 29–30)

There is, I suspect, not much room for matchboxes and macaroni here, and I fear that John Simson's tomb would not adequately traverse the vicissitudes of history. The sublime necessarily entails awe in response to grandeur. (Ironically, Kant himself maintained that the term did not apply to works of art. Only uncultivated nature could be truly sublime (2000: 136).)

The absolute, named here as empty, but desirable, is an object of pure intelligibility, the metaphysical foundation of Platonic idealism. For whom is it an object of desire? For philosophers, perhaps, but – and I have searched in vain among the vestiges of my own postmodern conscience for traces of its presence as a value – not, in my view, for cultural critics. Its attribution of independent existence to the absolute as idea is the reason, in a nutshell, why it is hard to believe that the sublime has any long-term value as an instrument of analysis for cultural criticism.

THE RETURN OF PSYCHOANALYSIS

Textually, Lyotard's discussions here are shot through with psychoanalytic models and terms, as my long quotation makes clear. What is at stake, he tells us, is an unconditional desire that is never fulfilled, just as it is in Lacan. 'The artistic is to the cultural as the real of desire is to the imaginary of demand.' The vocabulary of the second part of that sentence is taken straight from Lacan, as Lyotard himself would certainly have been the first to acknowledge. What, Lyotard asks, is the sublime 'it happens'? What happens, and in what circumstances? The occurrence, the unknown and unpredicted event, disarms thought and dismantles consciousness; it is 'what consciousness forgets in order to constitute itself' (1991: 90). Though the appropriation is inventive, the model here is Freud's. And Lyotard's paraphrase in 'What is Postmodernism?' of the inadequacy of the power to make truth present is directly Lacanian: he calls it there 'the withdrawal of the real' (1984: 79).

Lyotard's most sustained reflection on Kantian aesthetics takes place in *Lessons on the Analytic of the Sublime*, published in French in 1991. The overall project here is double: first to identify as a *differend* (a difference that cannot be resolved because no metalanguage embraces both terms) the distinction Kant makes between presentation and ideas, or imagination and reason. The effect is to render the unpresentable absolute incommunicable, undemonstrable, beyond proof and, in consequence, 'absolutely absent' (1994: 211). The second aspect of Lyotard's project is to read Kant attentively enough to call into question the traditional view of him as a philosopher above all of the subject. Thinking, Lyotard argues, is Kant's protagonist, not the subject, and in the case of the sublime, the capacity for thought hears the call of the unattainable absolute to think beyond what can be made present. The sublime constitutes a challenge to reach the unreachable, to defy in thought the limitations of thought's own finite character. Once again, Lyotard's vocabulary at this moment is revealing:

> In this regard the sublime feeling is only the irruption in and of thought of this deaf desire for limitlessness. Thinking takes 'action', it 'acts' the impossible, it subjectively 'realises' its omnipotence. It experiences pleasure in the Real.

'I ask the reader', he goes on, 'to forgive me for using terms of the idiom of Freud and Lacan to situate this violence' (1994: 55–6).

THE REAL ALTERNATIVE

I want to be as clear as I can about what I am suggesting here. This is not a criticism of Lyotard's Lacanian version of Kant. His appropriation of the third *Critique* is at once both scrupulous and inventive, and the intertextual result constitutes a rigorous account of what distinguishes modernism and the postmodern. Still less is it an accusation of plagiarism: Lyotard clearly knows what he borrows. On the contrary, my efforts to tease out his recurrent invocation of psychoanalysis, and especially the Lacanian real, represent a quest for the basis of an alternative way of understanding culture, without concessions, however negatively formulated, to hierarchy and transcendence. We have surely seen enough of critics as the high priests of culture to know that, if at this moment cultural criticism faces a challenge, it is to hold back on the assertion of personal tastes as eternal values, at least for long enough to follow through the implications, for our understanding of ourselves and our world, of the priority of the symbolic in permitting us to understand at all.

LYOTARD WITH LACAN

What, then, if we reread the combative 'Answering the Question: What is Postmodernism?', in many ways the most brilliant, and certainly the most provocative, of Lyotard's contributions to cultural criticism, in the light of the Lacanian real, rather than the Kantian sublime? That would give us a reading of postmodernism without recourse to a reification, however negative, of the unpresentable or a Romantic metaphysics of the absolute.

How much would change? In my view, very little that matters. Because we have no access to the real, visual realism is not truth,

Lyotard insists, but a way of 'ordering the visible' according to the formal rules of painting devised in Renaissance Italy. This perspective vision of the world reached its apotheosis in the Enlightenment, and its illusions remain effective still, wherever the project is to 'stabilize' the object represented. Realism positions objects in accordance with a point of view that makes them readily recognizable and, by this means, affirms the identity and confirms the knowledge of the viewing subject. Photography, film, television show us the world we think we know, generally from our accustomed point of view, and thus, at least in their mode of address, do not challenge us to re-examine our assumptions. The 'degree zero' of realism is pornography, which puts the object of the gaze – *as* object – just where the viewer wants it (Lyotard 1984: 74–5).

Modernist experimentation acknowledged 'the withdrawal of the real', repudiated the illusions of realism, and broke the rules in order to tell another kind of truth in painting. Its emphasis was ultimately self-referential, defining the signifier, not the object represented, as the material of art. The perspective organization of visual space gives way to a gradual flattening of the object against the picture plane, we might point out, supplementing Lyotard's brief but suggestive account. Both Whistler and Sickert, not to mention the pre-Raphaelite Dante Gabriel Rossetti, had already begun to compress and abstract space, and Matisse characteristically contracts it to show his figures confined in settings that seem to restrict them.

In the first decade of the twentieth century, modernism overtly and explicitly repudiates the Western tradition of fixed-point, monocular perspective, with its project of constructing for the spectator the illusion of what the eye actually sees. An insistence on the limitation of that single eye, the non-truth of the reality available to its specified point, generates fully-fledged Cubism, which displays the object from more than one point of view at once. This reintroduces the dimension of time. Seen from different angles at the same time, Cubist objects can seem to *move* as the eye follows the object from one angle to the next. The primary material of modernism is not the world, but paint on canvas. If the degree zero of realism is pornography, modernism's degree zero is abstract art, which makes no attempt to resemble anything.

What, then, Lyotard asks, is the postmodern? And the distinction he goes on to make seems to me profoundly suggestive in marking a difference useful to cultural criticism. While there is a strand of modernist painting and, indeed, of modernist fiction, that can be seen as nostalgic for the simulated truth of realism, for the real that cannot be made present, another contrasting strand celebrates the power of the signifier itself with 'jubilation'. No longer constrained by an obligation to reproduce what the eye sees, postmodernity discards the rules and searches for new forms that make of the work an 'event', an intervention which seeks retroactively the rules of what 'will have been done' (1984: 80–1). A festive radicalism defines the postmodern avant-garde.

DUCHAMP

The difference, Lyotard insists, between modern and postmodern is not merely chronological. Indeed, the most experimental work is always, in a sense, anachronistic: it comes, by definition, too soon for the public, or too late for its author (81). The postmodern is a variety of modernism, and its challenge to the rules constitutes a condition of modernism's existence in the first place. 'A work', he says, 'can become modern only if it is first postmodern. Postmodernism thus understood is not modernism at its end, but in its nascent state' (79).

In that respect, then, we might take as a prominent instance of the second of his categories, the cheeky affirmation of the new in the work of Marcel Duchamp. Duchamp's ready-made urinal, submitted for exhibition under the title *Fountain* in 1917, posed a challenge to the rules of art that was echoed, but not entirely superseded, by Piero Manzoni's cans of *Artist's Shit* in 1960, or Tracey Emin's *Bed* in 1999. 'You want reality in art?' all these artists seem to say. 'Here it is – for real.'

Read in the light of Lyotard's differend between 'regret and assay', as he puts it (80), or between nostalgia for the missing truth and celebration of the possibilities it liberates, Duchamp's work represents one 'assay' after another, each an assault on the shared values of the realist, perspective tradition. *The Large Glass*, Duchamp's work of 1915–23, mounts its puzzling assembly of oil, varnish, lead foil, wire and dust between two glass panels. The illusory transparency of the traditional perspective canvas-as-window-on-the-world gives way here to a real transparency. As a result, the viewer sees at one and the same time both the image itself and the little world of the gallery where the work stands.

While Duchamp was in the course of producing *The Large Glass*, he also constructed *The Small Glass* of 1918, which includes in its glass surface a Kodak lens. Brunelleschi's first panel, the inaugural painting of monocular, fixed-point perspective, held the viewer in place by means of a peep-hole the size of a lentil. The full name of *The Small Glass* parodies this coercive procedure: *To Be Looked at (the Other Side of the Glass) with One Eye, Close-to, for about an Hour.* It would be hard to better Thierry de Duve's intelligent, witty account of his own attempt to do as the title told him:

> I did this (not for an hour; patience has its limits), and the experience is very instructive. My eye riveted to the magnifying glass, I see – or rather I don't see – the work vanish from my visual field only for there to appear an inverted and reduced image of the gallery in the MoMA where the object is exhibited. A waiting period, uncomfortable and boring, begins. The revelation takes place when by chance another visitor passes who appears to me like a homunculus, upside down and in my former place, since I was initially on that side of the glass where the title/instruction was to be read. A missed encounter has just taken place – the glass serving as obstacle – between two spectators, he and I, two members of the public. Between the two of us the work was nothing but the instrument of this encounter. But since he occupies the place where I was, it is also with myself that I had this missed rendezvous to which I arrived late.
>
> (Duve 1999: 402–3)

In Duchamp's day, we might remember, the visual experience a peep-hole was likely to offer would not be a view of the Baptistry of San Giovanni nor, indeed, an art gallery and its visitors, but *What the Butler Saw*, the soft pornography available for a penny in a machine at the end of the pier. Duchamp's most shocking parody of the perspective tradition must surely be *Given:* 1) *The Waterfall,* 2) *The Illuminating Gas,* a work he produced between 1944 and 1966, now in the Philadelphia Museum of Art. Through two adjacent peepholes, the viewer sees a brick wall with a hole punched in it. This second, jagged hole reveals the naked figure of a woman represented in shallow perspective, spread-eagled for the benefit of the spectator, and brilliantly lit by a gas lamp she holds up incongruously in a daylight sylvan landscape.

Less scandalously, but with a high degree of invention, Duchamp puts space in motion in the *Roto-Reliefs (Optical Discs)* of 1935. The Kunsthalle in Bremen displays six assorted flat discs side by side, each about 20 cm in diameter, decorated with fine lines and circles in different colours. Made to spin mechanically, these lithographs produce a variety of bulging circles, alternating spirals and vortices, receding depths and projecting surfaces, creating the illusion of movement in three dimensions, without for an instant concealing the point that this is an illusion.

The object, to reverse Lyotard's analysis of realism, is consistently destabilized in Duchamp's work, or presented in such a way as to problematize the processes of recognition; it calls in question the identity and disturbs the 'knowledge' of the viewer. How, then, are we to read it? Is it playful, mischievous, designed to surprise and entertain? Or is there a serious imperative to be free of the constraints of the perspective tradition, to challenge the rules with a view to discovering in practice new forms that reveal what *will have been* the rules of their production? Or both? The 'postmodern' quality Lyotard's essay would allow us to find in Duchamp combines the exuberance of invention with the impulse to stretch the capabilities of art. There is no perceptible 'nostalgia for presence' here, no consolation of recognizable form (Lyotard 1984: 79–81). But nor is there simply a facile, gestural defiance of good taste. On the contrary, Duchamp's allusions to the tradition demand a good deal of the spectator.

THE POSTMODERN IN MODERNISM

Arguably, it was visual art that made the modernist running. But cinema was also the direct descendant of perspective painting, and modernist film, too, experimented in its own way with the presentation of visual space. Here and there cinema can be seen to challenge the emerging rules designed to perpetuate in moving pictures the illusion of three-dimensional reality. In *The Cabinet of Dr Caligari* (Robert Wiene, 1919), for instance, Expressionist sets appear to expand and contract the world the characters inhabit in line with their emotions, while unexpected angles and lines bent out of true distort domestic interiors and landscapes alike.

More exhilarating in its effects, Dziga Vertov's *Man With a Movie Camera* (1929) releases the camera from its conventional moorings at the eye-level of characters and audience to roam freely over and under the objects depicted on the screen. Split screens and superimposition produce impossible effects in a demonstration of the miracles film can perform. Meanwhile, in Hollywood in the 1930s Busby Berkeley's choreography opens up improbable spaces behind and beyond the stage that represents its official setting. These popular musicals celebrate the visual possibilities of cinema by showing dance formations from above, so that human bodies combine to make moving, abstract, kaleidoscopic patterns not unlike Duchamp's *Roto-Reliefs* of the same period.

Lyotard also mentions literature, but his only example of the post-modern is James Joyce. Modernist writing is generally less interested than visual art in the poetics of space, to confine ourselves for the sake of consistency to that one issue. Its primary concern is the inner workings of the human psyche, and it is no longer convinced by the 'realist' representation of feeling in linear patterns and the logical sequences of correct syntax. Developing the perspective insistence on vision as a transaction between viewer and object, modernism tends to treat place as an adjunct of consciousness in Leopold Bloom's Dublin (Joyce 1993) or Clarissa Dalloway's London (Woolf 1996). T. S. Eliot writes in 'Morning at the Window' of spatial relations distorted by weather conditions that might or might not be psychological as well: 'The brown waves of fog toss up to me/Twisted faces from the bottom of the street' (Eliot 1936: 27). Jean Rhys clearly draws on Expressionism when she writes in 1939 of houses as 'Tall cubes of darkness, with two lighted eyes at the top to sneer' (Rhys 1969: 28).

Luigi Pirandello's six fictitious characters, who insist on acting out the drama that ought to have been written for them, affirm a primacy for the signifier over everyday reality. As figments of the imagination, and immutable in consequence, they are more real, they allege, than the succession of illusions that constitute the beliefs of ordinary people. They claim to be more convincing, too, than their impersonations by the actors in the 'realist' tradition. Six Characters in Search of an Author, first performed in 1921, is the ancestor of all those interrogations of what's real identified as postmodern in Chapter 1.

It is hard, however, to name many modernist writers in English who celebrate the possibilities of the signifier with the wit of Pirandello's assault on the conventions, or Joyce's experimental verbal jubilation, unless, perhaps, in their distinct ways Gertrude Stein, or the playful Virginia Woolf of Orlando. A generation later, Samuel Beckett's bleak comedies would defy the rules and affirm the opacity of language with caustic festivity. But perhaps in reaction against the extravagant imagery of the Decadents, modernist literature is more commonly austere in tone and gloomy in content. If, however, it falls on the side of 'regret' more often than 'assay', that analysis only goes to show how suggestive Lyotard's distinction can be between modern and postmodern, or nostalgia and the jubilant avant-garde.

CONCEPTUAL ART

The postmodern as Lyotard defines it is variously impertinent, inventive and entertaining. Its allusions to the realist tradition invite us to reflect on the limitations of the form that betrayed its promise to deliver the truth in painting and fiction. And yet, as conceptual art increasingly severs its connection with the tradition, I seem to find that impudence alone doesn't do it for me. Instead, I am repeatedly drawn back to the texts which invoke realism with a difference: Citizen Kane (dir. Orson Welles, 1941); Toni Morrison's Beloved (1987); Tom Stoppard's Arcadia, first performed in 1993. (I shall have more to say about contemporary visual art and the tradition in the next chapter.)

Why is this? Not for their truth, certainly. What then? As a result of my own laziness? conservatism? social construction? Probably. But

Figure 8.1 In *L. H. O. O. Q.* Duchamp mocks the desire enlisted by
        traditional art. (The title has to be pronounced slowly in French,
        then translated.) (Marcel Duchamp, *L. H. O. O. Q.*, 1919.)

in addition, the thought that so often conceptual art seems to have given up on the *objet a*. What you see can be all you get. Celebrating the withdrawal of the real, the avant-garde often lacks or, indeed, mocks the desire enlisted by those pleasurable surfaces that kept the trace of a certain secret, even after they appeared to have divulged it (Figure 8.1).

In the three works I have named, we find out in the end the identity of Rosebud, uncover the memory screened by the survival of Beloved, or learn who the hermit turned out to be. But 'that's not it', we are entitled to respond. These instances of closure are variously something, or nothing much, no more in themselves than, say, a wooden reel. And for exactly that reason, all these texts allow me to go on supposing that behind the veil, or caught in its folds, perhaps, I just might find in them more than that, and more than they are, namely, the object-cause of desire.

Now, I wonder if the *objet a* was what Lyotard, the most Lacanian of philosophers, might have had in mind, when he was waylaid by the sublime, the absolute, and a trace of theology?

9

SUBLIME OR SUBLIMATION?

Towards a Theory of Culture

ŽIŽEK'S SUBLIME OBJECT

In the previous chapter I wanted to see how we might put to work a less Kantian and a more overtly Lacanian Lyotard. In this final one, we come back to Slavoj Žižek, the cultural analyst who claims to be most fully Lacanian. Žižek's work, ironically, is also 'postmodern' in Lyotard's terms, though Žižek himself would repudiate the adjective, claiming allegiance to Lyotard's great antagonist, Habermas, rather than to poststructuralism (Žižek 1989: 153).[1] As the Duchamp of cultural criticism, Žižek is more difficult to read than he seems at first glance, and more of an original theorist, I have suggested, than he claims. If Lacan authorizes Lyotard to reread Kant, Kant and Hegel license Žižek to reinterpret Lacan in the development of a theory of social antagonism.

As I indicated in Chapter 4, Žižek's incisive interpretation of social antagonism reproduces Lacan's increasing interest in the death drive, but with a difference. Žižek's insistence that the real is an absence, the void, no more than a retroactive psychical construct, brings him closer to German idealism than seems to me to match Lacan's repeated repudiations of the idealist view. For Lacan the real is there, but not there-for-a-subject. In Žižek's account, that the real is not there-for-a-subject means that the real is not there at all. The distinction between Lacan and Žižek here is perhaps no more than a nuance, but a nuance that turns out to make, I shall suggest, a world of difference.

THE IMPOSSIBLE *JOUISSANCE*

What fills the void of the real, Žižek goes on to argue, is the mirage of the sublime object. His sublime object takes the form of a fantasy-figure or a fetish, which masks the emptiness at the centre of the symbolic order. The sublime object promises an unearthly *jouissance*, the 'enjoyment' that would gratify the deadly, destructive drive. This *jouissance* cannot and must not be delivered. The wreck of the Titanic, marking the death of a certain ideal vision of the social order, is, he says, a sublime object, a 'materialization of the terrifying, impossible *jouissance*' (1989: 71). Stalin's 'man of steel' presents another sublime object, an invincible, indestructible creature, who constitutes the ideological justification of an appalling regime (145). Anti-Semitism projects onto the Jew the explanation of the actual antagonisms that divide what is supposed to be a unified and harmonious culture. The Jew constructed by anti-Semitism, another fantasy figure, blamed for fracturing this unity, embodies and at the same time disavows the structural impossibility of a unified society. 'It is as if', Žižek goes on, 'in the figure of the Jew this impossibility had acquired a positive, palpable existence – and that is why it marks the eruption of enjoyment in the social field' (126).

The 'negative pleasure' of the Kantian sublime permits Žižek to explain the simultaneous fascination and revulsion experienced in the encounter with the sublime object, that screen for the lost and, in Žižek's account, non-existent, real that is made to answer for what ideology cannot allow itself to acknowledge. The sublime gives him a brilliant and compelling insight into racism, for instance, as this example shows, and offers an original access to the inadequacies not only of Communism in former Eastern Europe, but of the West's highly prized but always disappointing liberal democracy.

THE SUBLIME AND SUBLIMATION

Žižek's position is Lacanian, however, only by a stretch of the imagination. Where Lyotard's Kant turns out to be a Lacanian, Žižek's Lacan becomes a Kantian as the sublime is conflated with sublimation. Here is what Žižek says:

> according to Lacan, a sublime object is an ordinary, everyday object which, quite by chance, finds itself occupying the place of what he calls *das Ding*, the impossible-real object of desire. The sublime object is 'an object elevated to the level of *das Ding*.' It is its structural place – the fact that it occupies the sacred/forbidden place of *jouissance* – and not its intrinsic qualities that confers on it its sublimity.
>
> (Žižek 1989: 194)

This is not an incidental quotation in *The Sublime Object of Ideology*. Indeed, Žižek invokes it more than once (71) and continues to quote it in an essay first published ten years later (Žižek 1999b: 297–8). What Lacan actually says, both in French and in English, is this: 'the most general formula that I can give you of *sublimation* is the following: it raises an object . . . to the dignity of the Thing' (Lacan 1986: 133; 1992: 112; my emphasis).

Sublime: sublimation. The distinction is barely perceptible in English: two additional syllables, a whisper of difference. In French to sublimate is *sublimer*. But the etymology of the two words is not the same. Sublimity is in the first instance a measure of height: *sub limen*, up to the lintel above the door. It means lofty, towering, belonging to the highest regions, however much its postmodern usage renders this association ironic. And if the *limen* the sublime measures up to is also a threshold, a limit, so much the better, since the Kantian sublime is the place where imagination recoils, turns back, acknowledging its own inadequacy, and seeks the help of reason, the supersensible faculty. Sublimation, by contrast, is the process of converting a solid direct to a gas or, in Freud's metaphorical usage, a sexual drive to a socially acceptable project. There would be no pun in Freud's German to connect his *Sublimierung* with Kant's *Erhabene*.

Lacan himself comments momentarily on the overlap between the two words in French, which may, he says, be more than coincidental: 'We haven't yet extracted from the Kantian definition of the sublime all the substance we might. The conjunction of this term with that of sublimation is probably not simply an accident nor simply homonymic' (1992: 301). But his interest throughout *Seminar 7* is in the beautiful, which Kant consistently associates with pleasure and satisfaction. Lacan's version of sublimation satisfies the drive without recourse to neurosis. He takes no further steps in *Seminar 7* to extract any substance at all from the sublime. When he reaches the question of Kant's distinction between the sublime and the beautiful, he passes the topic on to someone else to discuss, and then reverts to his own concern with the beautiful for the remainder of the seminar (286–7).

Žižek's sublime object, by contrast, is neither beautiful, nor pleasurable and satisfying. On the contrary, as the symptom of an apparently universal pathology, the sublime object is at worst a materialization of forbidden *jouissance*, and at best no more than a 'mask of death' (1999a: 159).

THE PLEASURE PRINCIPLE

What difference does Žižek make by his intertextual conjunction of psychoanalytic sublimation with the Kantian sublime? Lacan's *Seminar 7* concerns the ethical implications of psychoanalysis. The question it asks is what psychoanalysis offers as its outcome for the analysand. Given that 'the goods' – duty, self-sacrifice, the conventional virtues – solve nothing, what would it mean to be free from the symptom, which always conceals the drive towards the Thing? How, in other words, can we avoid, on the one hand, the naked aggressivity that represents the direct projection outwards of the death drive and, on the other, the effect of repression, the symptom's deception, by which neurosis promises its own pathological version of satisfaction?

It is in answer to the question how to avoid pathology that Lacan impels us not to give ground relative to our desire (1992: 319). His instance of the tragic outcome of this ethic is Antigone, whose bond with her brother impels her to defy Creon's law, knowing that the consequence is to be walled up alive in her own tomb. The rest of us, less heroic, may be less ready to venture beyond everything we think we know, or more eager to postpone the moment, since we are all required to rejoin the real in the end. For us, what is deadly in desire must be acknowledged, but may also be tamed, pacified, fenced off, as a way of living with – or, indeed, surviving – the effects of that uncompromising commitment. The beautiful, then, is the acceptable barrier to 'the unspeakable field of radical desire that is the field of absolute destruction' (216).

People are speaking beings, organisms-in-culture, able to find themselves fully at home neither in the organic real nor in the symbolic order. The Thing beckons with the promise of gratification at the level of the real, but the price we should pay for such *jouissance* would be the dissolution of the subject. Conversely, the symbolic order, the Other which constitutes us as subjects, is empty; it cannot give a satisfaction it does not possess. Sublimation in Lacan's account offers a way of inhabiting the symbolic without submission to the exorbitant demands of the ferocious moral Law. Sublimation, which gratifies without repression, involves the pleasure principle.

FREUD'S THEORY OF SUBLIMATION

Modernity has not given sublimation high marks. Our epoch tends to prefer sex. In order to justify this preference, it draws on a reading of Freud to form what Michel Foucault dismisses as 'the repressive hypothesis' that we have been unhealthily deprived of gratification (1979). In consequence, the idea of an alternative has not seemed particularly attractive. Sublimation appears repeatedly in Freud's work from 1905 onwards as a diversion of part of the sexual drive towards other aims. Under the influence of the ego, he argues, people relinquish a proportion of organic satisfaction in favour of culturally acceptable activities. Art is the effect of sublimation.

At times Freud displays all the scepticism of science in his depiction of the artist. 'He' (artists are characteristically male, of course, in Freud) is probably exceptionally driven, but also exceptionally socially inept. What he wants is what all men want: glory, power and the love of women. But when he fails to secure any of them, the artist retreats into fantasy, imagines the satisfaction he seeks. Whereas most people in these circumstances would have to make do with their meagre day-dreams, however, the artist, Freud explains, is especially good at making his fantasies public in acceptable forms, while disguising their origins. Artists convert imagination into works of art. By means of this skill, they go on to acquire glory, power and the love of women in the process, thus securing their objectives after all, but by another route (Freud 1976: 423–4).

Elsewhere, however, Freud's account is more elegiac. Something in the nature of the sexual drive, he proposes, is incompatible with civilization, so that for human beings, divorced by culture from their organic origins, perfect sexual gratification is not possible. But para-doxically, the pleasure that culture withholds in this way reappears in culture itself by means of sublimation:

> The very incapacity of the sexual instinct to yield complete satisfac-tion as soon as it submits to the first demands of civilization becomes the source, however, of the noblest cultural achievements which are brought into being by ever more extensive sublimation of its instinc-tual components. For what motive would men have for putting sexual instinctual forces to other uses if, by any distribution of those forces, they could obtain fully satisfying pleasure?
>
> (Freud 1977a: 259)

That element of lack in the sexual relation was to reappear in Lacan's account of unconscious desire as indestructible and insatiable, and in his repeated insistence in Seminar 20 that there was no sexual relation (rapport). But what complicates the issue further is Freud's increasing conviction after the First World War that there are two drives, the libido on the one hand, and the death drive on the other. While Beyond the Pleasure Principle, published in 1920, holds them apart only with some degree of uncertainty, Civilization and its Discontents, ten years later, insists on the distinction and pays renewed attention to the dangerous capabilities of the death drive. Externalized, it leads to cruelty and brutality towards others; internalized, it produces the self-destructive and voracious superego, conscience, an exorbitant sense of moral obligation that can never be fully met, and which therefore creates unending anxiety: 'Every renunciation of instinct now becomes a dynamic source of conscience and every fresh renunciation increases the latter's severity and intolerance' (Freud 1985a: 321). Civilization is necessary as a defence against unqualified aggressivity, but its effects remain disappointing. Among its discontents we must include the self-denying, self-excoriating ethical imperatives of the superego, aggression itself by another name.

LACAN'S THEORY OF SUBLIMATION

Tracing a path through Freud's own widely distributed observations, Lacan repudiates the binary opposition Freud holds on to so precariously between the libido and death: for Lacan the drive is both sexual and deadly, at once life-giving and destructive. In *Seminar 7* sexual desire is not the central problem. Sex, Lacan says, is fine in its way, but you can't count on it:

> It is doubtless possible to achieve for a single moment in this act something which enables one human being to be for another in the place that is both living and dead of the Thing. In this act and only at this moment, he may simulate with his flesh the consummation of what he is not under any circumstances. But even if the possibility of this consummation is polarizing and central, it cannot be considered timely.
>
> (Lacan 1992: 300)

Sex 'simulates' the impossible *jouissance*, the encounter with the Thing, but does not in any circumstances enact it.

Meanwhile, however, *Seminar 7* is less concerned about sex than death. For Lacan sex was never an origin: instead, it merely 'occupies', like an invading army, the field of desire (1977: 287), which is brought into being with the loss of the real entailed in our subjection to the symbolic order. In Lacan's account, sublimation includes romantic love; there is no conflict between sublimation and sex; on the contrary, sex involves the pleasurable signifier. Sublimation rails off the impossible encounter with the engulfing Thing, not the pleasures of sex.

A product of his time, however, in the late 1950s and early 1960s, when the world held its breath as two superpowers threatened each other with nuclear annihilation, Lacan became increasingly preoccupied by the death drive, and specifically its expression in the capacity of human beings to destroy their world with weapons of mass destruction. Sublimation pacifies the drive without pathology and without destruction.

There are two possible barriers between the subject and the object of the drive, two ways to keep at bay the death-dealing and vital Thing: on the one hand, the superego; on the other, sublimation. True to Freud, Lacan finds the superego, 'obscene', 'ferocious' and 'morbid' (1992: 7). The more we concede to this 'parasite', the more it demands of us, he argues (302). Its ideals are 'the goods': conventional values, 'family goods, domestic goods . . . the goods of our trade or our profession, the goods of the city, etc'. But psychoanalysis is not there, Lacan insists, to support the bourgeois dream, with its puritanical demands for human sacrifice (303).

If, then, we refuse the goods, one option is to go willingly with Antigone, into a heroic region beyond pleasure, a world of total dispossession, the unearthly place of the drive itself. In the meantime, sublimation promises pleasure at the level of the signifier – including the pleasure offered by the plays of Sophocles, and not least, of course, *Antigone*. Sublimation, then, is the 'true' barrier between us and absolute destruction, preferable to the goods because beauty 'gets closer' to the Thing (216–17). The pleasure principle presents the beautiful as capable of alluding to the Thing, revealing the nature of the drive, and in the process offering a gratification that differs from its aim (111, 293).

There is nothing sentimental or escapist about the beautiful in Lacan. On the contrary, 'the beautiful is closer to evil than to the good' (217). Moreover, it is 'precisely the function of the beautiful to reveal to us the site of man's relationship to his own death, and to reveal it to us only in a blinding flash' (295). By encircling the void, which marks the place of the real that is lost to the subject, culture exercises the creative aspect of the drive to make allusions at the level of the symbolic to the inaccessible Thing, which is itself beyond pleasure. In culture the symbol comes between us and the enticing, terrifying, dangerous object of the drive.

ŽIŽEK OR LACAN?

To be as clear as possible, I do not want to say that Žižek's appropriation of Lacan and his introduction of the sublime are illegitimate. Intertextuality leads beyond mere imitation. In the same way as Lacan rereads Freud to create a psychoanalysis Freudians might not recognize, Žižek creates a Lacan who is not wholly Lacanian. Both, of course, are exercising the creative capabilities of sublimation in the process.

Besides, *Seminar 7* includes much that would support Žižek's analysis of human nature as grounded in antagonism. Allusions to the threat of nuclear weapons thread their way through *Seminar 7*. Just as Freud writes *Beyond the Pleasure Principle* in 1920, in the immediate aftermath of the First World War, *Seminar 7* rewrites (or, at least, respeaks) Freud's text forty years later, in the full recognition of a new and unprecedented potential for apocalyptic destructiveness developed and ready for human use (104–5, cf. 324–5). Lacan even manages to uncover an allusion to modern warfare in one of the choruses of *Antigone* (266).

The Thing is undeniably antagonistic. It is even, in its own way, sublime. Lacan does not say so, but he characterizes it as 'impossible for us to imagine' (125); it is certainly unpresentable. Lyotard sees the connection, though he does not attribute it to Lacan himself (1991: 33). There is in *Seminar 7*, however, no sublime object, unreasonably elevated to the dignity of the Thing, no fetish, no fantasy offering a focus for antagonism. On the contrary, while the Thing is best acknowledged, it is also preferable that it should be veiled by the signifier. And the signifier gives pleasure.

To secure the sublime object of ideology, Žižek sacrifices the version of sublimation that explains the existence of culture. If Žižek offers on the basis of Lacan a theory of human nature, what Lacan offers on the basis of Freud is a theory of human culture as the only hope of a rapprochement between the symbolic and the real.

Lacan insists on the gap between the real and the signifier. Lyotard adapts Lacan, to arrive at an idealist gap between the idea and the signifier, in the light of the sublime. Žižek denies the existence of the real but places the sublime object at the heart of culture.

Paradoxically, however, this leads him to ignore the capacity of the signifier to give pleasure – though he demonstrates it in his own extremely pleasurable writing over and over again. Only Lacan retains a substantial positivity that the signifier cannot master, an unknown region which we encounter in fear and trembling, but with no trace of theology. Žižek says you have to go through the fantasy to the void; Lacan says you can do that – but in the meantime, you can make things.

Making things is what culture consists of, given that the things in question include pots, beads, stories, paintings, photographs, films, essays and academic books. This is the material of cultural criticism, and only Lacan, who largely ignores the Kantian sublime, gives us a theoretical explanation of its existence.

MODERNISM REVISITED

The test of a theory must be what it is able to achieve in practice. Suppose, then, that we were to rewrite yet again Lyotard's compelling story of the rejection of realism in favour of the modern and the postmodern, this time in the light of Lacan's account of sublimation. How would it look?

Pots, temples, perspective images were all forms of the beautiful, all ways, Lacan argued, of encircling emptiness, and thereby alluding to the Thing in the lost but unforgettable real. (Note again that none of these would have been *sublime* for Kant, who explicitly excludes from his definition all made objects, even St Peter's in Rome (2000: 136).) Modernism rejects perspective in particular, however, and the realist values it represents in general, as illusions, conjuring tricks designed to reassure the subject that it possesses the truth about the objects of its knowledge. Modernism emphasizes the signifier, whether in the spirit of 'regret' for the irrecoverable truth or 'jubilation' at its creative possibilities. Modern painting first flattens space, pushing increasingly towards abstraction and then, a generation later, goes on to find ways of invoking the missing third dimension at the level of the picture plane itself. Jackson Pollock, for instance, superimposes layer upon layer of paint until the pictorial surface projects forwards towards the viewer. He often incorporates small objects –

nails, tacks, buttons, coins – into the paint itself. Conversely, Lucio Fontana tears open his monochrome canvasses, permitting a glimpse of what is *not* there beyond the signifying exterior. ⬦

Other forms repudiate painting itself. What is Duchamp's *Fountain*? Not a sculpture, certainly, but a work in three dimensions by a painter challenging the hanging committee of the New York Independents to reconsider, among other issues, the conventional generic divisions within what constituted art (Duve 1999: 147–54). Subsequently Donald Judd's minimalist boxes specifically enclose space, while repudiating any decorative prettiness. In his *Untitled*, 1988, now in Brussels, ten boxes, one above the other, are evenly spaced vertically against the wall, the upper and lower surfaces made of copper, so that they reflect their surroundings. Because of the reflections, and depending on the light, some appear solid, others open. More austere still, Sol LeWitt's open structures are no more than frames – cubes, rectangles, cellular forms – indicating where an enclosure might be, and in the process marking off areas of vacancy.

Meanwhile, large-scale installations permit access, inviting the spectator into the space they frame, but often problematize as they do so. Jean Dubuffet's *Le Jardin d'hiver* (Musée d'Art Moderne, Paris, 1968–70) lures us into a kind of igloo, white inside, but with the black lines that op art made familiar drawn on the 'walls' and 'floor'. The lining of the igloo is everywhere uneven, the floor at different levels, the surfaces of 'walls' and 'ceiling' lumpy, curved, unpredictable, and the black lines apparently randomly spaced, but continuous. After a moment or two, the surfaces seem to move in response to our stare, and the fixed point of the motionless viewer becomes uncertain, unstable, relative. We no longer master the space art contains: instead, we are inside it, ourselves contained, framed.

In a different way, *Labyrinth: My Mother's Album* by Ilya and Emilia Kabakov (1990, Tate Modern) draws the viewer into a succession of dimly lit corridors lined with photographs of a life in Soviet Russia. There is a sound of chanting. As we reach the heart of the labyrinth, the voice is louder. There is nothing to see, however, but a small square room with what looks like builders' rubble. The truth we have sought at the heart of the work, if truth it is, turns out to be disappointing, banal remnants, junk.

GHOST

Examples could be endlessly multiplied, but one artist's installations bear a unique relation to Lacan's account of art's impulse to enclose emptiness. Rachel Whiteread makes casts of vacant spaces, renders substantial and palpable the areas under beds, tables and chairs, inside wardrobes, below staircases, on landings. *Ghost*, produced in 1990, solidifies the empty space within a room in a Victorian house. The effect verges on the uncanny.

In 1993 Whiteread cast the inside of a whole house in the East End of London, and left the concrete cast in place after the house, and the terrace of which it formed an unexceptional part, had been demolished. Standing alone, with its blind windows, in a newly-turfed grass area beside the road, the work exerted a desolate fascination (Figure 9.1). In *The Independent* on 2 November 1993 Andrew Graham-Dixon wrote:

> *House* is a paradox made concrete since it is a monument made out of void space, a thing constructed out of the absence of things. Being a dwelling in which it is not possible to dwell, a building that you cannot enter, it has the character of a tantalus. It is both a relic and a prompt to the imagination (Who lived here? What did they do? What did they feel?) as well as a sculpture that is charged with a deep sense of loss.

Loss, indeed, was the condition of its construction, since *House* came into existence only on condition of the demolition of the dwelling from which it was cast. The enthusiasm of the art-world and most of the press for the work failed to soften the resolve of the local council to be rid of it, and *House* itself was demolished only months after its initial construction. So in the end it was doubly missing, twice lost.

There was an embarrassing quality to *House*, as if we became privy to something not usually displayed, a personal, private domesticity made awkwardly public. And yet there was to see, after all, nothing but vacancy, impossibly congealed, literally set in concrete. *House* can be read as an exercise in nostalgia for Victorian London, as a

Figure 9.1 Rachel Whiteread's *House* exerted a desolate fascination.
(Rachel Whiteread, *House*, 1993).

political statement about the ironies of inner-city housing policies, or as a demonstration of the endless inventiveness of contemporary art. It also testifies to the possibility of absence made present, the space that represents the only way of recording the lost real at once made visible and barred. There was no *access* to *House*, and yet what you saw was what you got. It concealed, in every sense, nothing.

The smaller *Ghost*, however, Whiteread's cast of a single room, still stands in the Saatchi Gallery. To come upon it without expectations, as I did the first time, is to encounter an enigma, a shape both mysterious and oddly familiar, that gradually declares itself a room, but inside-out. The overall impression of the white plaster, with its moulded incisions made by skirting boards and picture rails is classical, monumental, but an incongruous fireplace projects oddly outwards, while electric sockets are recorded as cavities. The sash windows are blank, inverted, the door panels reversed. You can't, of course, get in.

It offers itself to no particular point of view. The work bears a close resemblance, necessarily, to the space it was cast from, but

Ghost's visibility now depends on the removal of the cast from the room as it was then. Literally imprinted by its own past, *Ghost* thus inscribes a vanished moment in the present, but as a kind of resurrection. The installation has, in this way, no tense. White, lifeless, spectral, as its name indicates, *Ghost* is simultaneously substantial and signifying. It appears at the same time strangely vulnerable without the shell that was the original condition of its existence. The effect is hard to define: sad, solemn, and yet, paradoxically, witty and exhilarating. Ironically, the process of its construction represents the precise reversal of sublimation in its literal, chemical sense: Whiteread turns gases directly into solids.

Only art's break with realism makes *Ghost* possible. And yet an awareness of the perspective tradition still informs this work, which so improbably monumentalizes the empty spaces that were the location of desire in the classic works of the Western tradition. In that sense, too, *Ghost* at once pays tribute to the past and bears witness to art's capacity to make new forms, discovering in the process Lyotard's rules of what has been done.

The study of popular culture can easily give the impression that nothing changes. Hollywood genres, endlessly repeated to ensure commercial success, or soap operas, more 'daring' in their subject matter but profoundly conservative in form, might seem to support a version of cultural determinism. This would be a false impression. I argued in Chapter 1 that Hollywood itself pushes at and beyond the limits of predictability. Lyotard's point, however, is that we (also) need the avant-garde, where challenges to the rules are themselves the rule, and where culture sets out to advance into unmapped spaces. That sphere is currently claimed most evidently by visual art. Whiteread's casts expand the range of culture in a specific and curiously Lacanian way, embodying the emptiness that alludes in representation to the lost real and the impossible Thing which haunt the speaking being.

MALONE DIES

A generation earlier, and contemporary with Lacan himself, Samuel Beckett invokes the unknowable real in a different way. Beckett's novel, *Malone Dies*, opens with the words, 'I shall soon be quite dead at last in spite of all' (Beckett 1994: 179). Malone is resigned to the inevitability of death, although he would prefer it to take place without struggle. 'Throes', he observes laconically, 'are the only trouble, I must be on my guard against throes' (179–80). First published in French in 1951, and translated into English by the author in 1956, *Malone Dies* anticipates some of the concerns of Lacan's *Seminar 7*, though in a manner entirely characteristic of its own author.

The novel is also characteristic of its moment. Lacan's exemplary text, *Antigone*, shows its protagonist refusing to give ground relative to her desire. Organically linked to her dead brother, as to no other human being (a husband or a child would be replaceable, she says, but her mother and father are dead: she can have no new brothers), Antigone insists on carrying out his burial rites, contrary to Creon's law. Because she accepts the penalty of living burial, Antigone's 'incarnation' of the death drive is heroic (Lacan 1992: 282). Oedipus, meanwhile, enters the zone between life and death because he too has insisted on following his own desire, in this instance, 'to know the last word on desire'. Everyone else tries in vain to discourage him from pressing his questions about who he is, but he persists. Oedipus dies cursing, unreconciled to the goods. On the other hand, King Lear, the irascible old man who does not give up on his desire either, represents a 'derisory' version of the same commitment (1992: 310). The 'old fool' thinks he can go into the same zone with everyone's agreement – and 'makes the earth and ocean echo' with his imprecations, because he fails to grasp that this is a place of dispossession (1992: 309–10)

Malone, however, is a protagonist for our own ironic time. There is nothing remotely heroic about Malone except his refusal of the goods. Neither stoical nor serene, Malone makes no concessions whatever to the moral law: 'Let me say before I go any further that I forgive nobody. I wish them all an atrocious life and then the fires and ice of hell and in the execrable generations to come an honoured name' (Beckett 1994: 180).

Malone inhabits the zone between life and death alone in an isolated room that he cannot quite locate. Could it be 'one of heaven's mansions' perhaps? He thinks not (184). It seems to be in an ordinary house. There remains a doubt, however. Is it, perhaps, already the vault, and the space he thinks of as the street outside no more than a trench in a kind of catacomb (219)? The progressive loss of sensation is registered in terms of this enigmatic space. At one stage the light ceases to come through the window: it subsists out there, glittering, but it does not come in, leaving the room in shadow – no, not even shadow, but 'a kind of leaden light that makes no shadow', a colourless 'grey incandescence' (221). Is the room, after all, merely inside his head, its six planes made of bone? The planes blanch, whiten (222–3).

Finally,

> The ceiling rises and falls, rises and falls, rhythmically, as when I was a foetus . . . . I am being given, if I may venture the expression, birth to into death, such is my impression. The feet are clear already, of the great cunt of existence. Favourable presentation I trust. My head will be the last to die. Haul in your hands. I can't . . . . That is the end of me. I shall say no more.
>
> (285)

Death reverses the process of birth, as this 'old foetus' prepares to 'land head-foremost mewling in the charnel-house' (226).

To die is to be reunited with the real we came from, but the living Malone is at home neither as an organism, in the flesh, nor at the level of the signifier. 'All my senses are trained full on me, me. Dark and silent and stale, I am no prey for them. I am far from the sounds of blood and breath' (186). Malone is not his body. On the other hand, he is not a consciousness either: thought seeks him out, 'as it always has, where I am not to be found' (187). The space he inhabits, however unstable, ill-defined, seems easier to specify than his identity.

It is to the signifier, however, that Malone turns to keep his distance from the real, physical process of dying. He tells – and then writes in an exercise book – stories. The first effort, in the manner of a folk-tale or a *Bildungsroman*, bores him (not without reason). As his body disintegrates, however, the stories get better, the parodies of existing genres more pronounced. One of them recounts how, in the asylum, the ageing Macmann couples with his even older keeper, Moll. They are initially incapable,

> but far from losing heart, they warmed to their work. And though both were completely impotent they finally succeeded, summoning to their aid all the resources of the skin, the mucus and the imagination, in striking from their dry and feeble clips a kind of sombre gratification.
>
> (261)

In this grotesque love story Malone keeps organism and signifier remorselessly distinct, while bringing them into reciprocal relation with each other. Copulation, it turns out, will have an improving effect on Macmann's language skills, as he gradually learns when to utter 'the yesses, noes, mores and enoughs that keep love alive' (261). He discovers the pleasure of reading in response to Moll's inflammatory love letters; he himself begins to write very bad poems.

Malone Dies ends, as it must, with the signifier, not the real. But it reaches no closure. Malone is in the process of recounting the story of a picnic for the inmates of the asylum, like a grotesque Sunday-School outing, arranged by their benefactor, Lady Pedal, when the text peters out.

Is there anything uplifting here? Not really. But there is comedy, and it pacifies. In the absence of heroism, there is at least dedication, if only in Malone's resolute contempt for the good death. Above all, there is pleasure in the grim wit of Beckett's prose. What are verbal dexterity, stories, jokes, satire, parody, and satirical excoriation itself, after all, but an affirmation of the signifier in the face of the real? And isn't that exactly what, as organisms-in-culture, we speaking beings are good at?

A THEORY OF CULTURE?

Lacan's account of sublimation offers a way of understanding the pleasures the signifier offers the speaking being, without reducing culture to something else: ethical instruction, ideological control, or scripted determinism. Aspects of culture may at a specific moment represent any or all of these. In itself, however, culture does not make us better or worse. If it subjects people, it does not exclude the possibility of resistance. It does not do away with our discontents, but it offers to engage with them while finding a focus for desire. And to the attentive interpreter, culture can in addition tell more than it thinks it knows about who and what we are.

FURTHER READING

GENERAL

My best advice is to distrust all introductions (even mine!). Interpretations always select, and they may not select exactly those insights that would enable you to put together a new and challenging case. What's more, some secondary sources are just plain wrong.

In what follows, I recommend secondary sources very sparingly indeed, and try to point to passages of the primary texts that are more entertaining and less impenetrable than others. (Perhaps one day someone will put them together in a reader.) But if, after all, you still want a general introduction to the field, what can I recommend but my own *Poststructuralism: A Very Short Introduction* (2002b)? (It really is very short.)

LACAN

In addition to the general difficulty of French theory, there is an extra problem in reading Lacan. He was addressing psychoanalysts in the first instance, and he expected them to listen with the close attention due to their analysands. In the seminars, which we derive from tapes and notes, he therefore assumed the right to digress, follow associations without announcing very clearly when he was resuming his main theme for the week, make puns (in French, but not necessarily with a view to being intelligible in translation) and generally cover his tracks in just the way an analysand might. His written texts are on the whole even more demanding, and in much the same kinds of ways.

So you might need an introduction. Malcolm Bowie does justice to Lacan's complexity, but without simply reproducing it (1991). Dylan Evans's *Dictionary* is exactly that, and very thorough (1996). He gives the references which demonstrate Lacan's changing use of terms, and the best way to use his book is to follow them up. Borch-Jacobsen is harder, but highly intelligent (1991). And Shepherdson explains clearly why psychoanalysis is incompatible with mind–body dualism (2000).

After that, why not try the texts themselves? In this book I draw particularly on *Seminar 7, The Ethics of Psychoanalysis* (1992). This *is* about ethics, in a rather unexpected way, but it's much *more* about the relationship between desire and culture. Most of the argument about art encircling emptiness occurs in a seminar rather unhelpfully entitled 'Marginal Comments' (pp. 128–38). The following seminar gives a psychoanalytic account of courtly love (139–54). If you know the *Antigone* of Sophocles, Lacan's reading is very powerful and surprisingly textual (241–87). (If you don't know the play, it's easy to read, and short.) The final seminar in that volume is vintage Lacan (311–25) and much cited by Žižek. The account of the gaze as *objet a* in *Seminar 11* is hard, but has become a classic (1979: 65–119). So has 'The Signification of the Phallus', because it tells the story of language and desire (1977: 281–91). Lacan registers his late views on language and sex in 'To Jakobson'. This has lucid intervals, but don't expect rational exposition (1998: 14–25).

FREUD

Lacan makes a lot more sense if you are already familiar with Freud, who writes quite differently. The problem here is that it's all deceptively lucid, so that, when the argument doesn't hold, we feel it must be our fault. Not always! Here the introductions are all too likely to lead you off in a schematic direction that won't help at all. And you don't need them. The case histories make good reading, especially Freud 1974 and 1977b. 'The "Uncanny"' has exerted a good deal of influence on cultural criticism (1985b). For the drives see 'Instincts and their Vicissitudes' (1984: 105–38).

LYOTARD

My other major influence in this book has been Jean-François Lyotard, who can be extremely pleasurable to read. If you want an introduction, Bill

Readings is good (1991). But the texts themselves are even better. 'Can Thought Go On Without a Body?' is perfectly straightforward (and the answer is 'no') (1991: 8–23). 'A Postmodern Fable' combines theory with science fiction (as, of course, does much science fiction) (1997: 83–101). 'Answering the Question: What is Postmodernism?' is packed with allusions and can seem quite hard, but if you've followed my arguments in this book, you shouldn't have much trouble with it (1984: 71–82).

BUTLER

To make up your own mind about Judith Butler, read the Preface to the first edition of *Gender Trouble* (1999: xxvii–xxxiii) and then the first chapter (3–44). See whether you think the Introduction to *Bodies that Matter* resolves the question of the relationship between between the body and gender to your satisfaction (1993: 1–23). 'Critically Queer' has been widely anthologized, which suggests that it is equally widely admired (223–42). It is certainly clearer than other parts of the book. 'Arguing with the Real' takes issue with Žižek, rather than Lacan (187–222). Oddly enough, the essay I like best in *Bodies that Matter* gives a reading of Nella Larsen's novel, *Passing* (167–85). Butler is very good on the political possibilities of speech-act theory in *Excitable Speech* (1997).

ŽIŽEK

Žižek has written a great deal, all of it in varying ways challenging and entertaining. *The Žižek Reader* is as good a place to start as any, and would allow you to assess his claims to represent Lacan (1999b: 11–36), his version of Lacan's account of courtly love (148–73) and his relationship to Hegel (225–50). It also includes a bibliography up to 1998, though its proleptic details on *The Ticklish Subject* were premature in the event.

NOTES

WHAT'S REAL?

1 It would not be entirely anachronistic to see the film as self-aware in this respect. The Cole Porter musical, *Les Girls* (dir. George Cukor, 1957), depends on a conflict between two accounts of what 'really' happened, and the happy ending is made possible when a third version of the story exonerates everyone. Ironically, however, this third version is presented as quite possibly the least trustworthy. At intervals an unmotivated figure appears in the crowd wearing a sandwich board with the words 'What is truth'. On the other hand, what is at stake here is the difficulty of finding a reliable narrator; truth is not seen as unknowable *in principle*.

2 Thurber's hero is escaping from an overbearing wife; in his final fantasy he faces a firing squad – heroically, of course (Thurber 1953).

3 At first glance, *The Neverending Story* (Wolfgang Petersen, 1984) looks like a prototype. This disarming children's movie, full of quaint characters, including a racing snail and a love-dragon, pulls its reader-protagonist into the action of the story itself. Only Bastian, it turns out, can save the land of Fantasia from the encroaching, destructive Nothing. But Bastian has just lost his mother and is sinking into sadness until this encounter with 'the world of human fantasies' gives him hope. In the end, psychological allegory deflects the question of what's real.

4 For a brilliant reading of *Last Action Hero*, and the role of Death in it, see Mallin 1999.

PSYCHOANALYSIS BEYOND IDEALISM

1 Descartes's word, *âme*, could be translated as 'soul' or 'mind'. Neither quite captures the ambiguity of the French term.
2 The English translation unhelpfully gives *Trieb* (drive) as instinct, thus confusing the issues slightly. Freud's German allowed him to distinguish between *Trieb* and *Instinkt*.

ŽIŽEK AGAINST LACAN

1 I agree, however, with Žižek's point that the main political casualty of 9/11 was Europe: 'the result of September 11 is an unprecedented strengthening of American hegemony, in all its aspects. Europe succumbed to a kind of ideologico-political blackmail by the US: "What is now at stake are no longer different economical or political choices, but our very survival – in the war of terrorism, you are either with us or against us". . . . In the name of the "war on terrorism", a certain positive vision of global political relations is silently imposed on us Europeans' (2002: 144–5). To the shame of the British government, after an initial attempt to invoke the United Nations, it simply adopted America's world picture, radically diminishing in the process the possibility of an independent Europe.

CULTURE'S MAGIC CIRCLE

1 For a discussion of the possible relationship between these 'standing' effigies and Hermione's 'statue' in *The Winter's Tale*, see Belsey 1999: 111–20.

THE REAL AND THE SUBLIME

1 Unusually, Thierry de Duve bravely opts for the beautiful as the framework for a compelling argument about the political implications of modernism (Duve 1999).
2 A philosophical case could be made for tracing the Lacanian real to Kant's things-in-themselves, and connecting things-in-themselves with uncultivated nature and the sublime. But Eagleton does not make it,

perhaps because he was aware that Lacan himself would not have accepted it (see p. 62, this volume).

SUBLIME OR SUBLIMATION?

1 This allegiance appears to have shifted. More recently Žižek writes of 'the utter impotence of Habermasian ethics' (2002: 34).

REFERENCES

Alberti, Leon Battista (1991) *On Painting*, ed. Martin Kemp, Harmondsworth: Penguin.

Appignanesi, Lisa and John Forrester (1992) *Freud's Women*, London: Weidenfeld & Nicolson.

Augustine (1912) *Confessions*, trans. William Watts, 2 vols, The Loeb Classical Library, London: William Heinemann, vol. 1.

Austen, Jane (1996) *Pride and Prejudice*, ed. Vivien Jones, Harmondsworth: Penguin.

Barnes, Julian (1998) *England, England*, London: Jonathan Cape.

Barthes, Roland (1975) *S/Z*, trans. Richard Miller, London: Jonathan Cape.

—— (1976) *The Pleasure of the Text*, trans. Richard Miller, London: Jonathan Cape.

—— (1982) *Camera Lucida: Reflections on Photography*, trans. Richard Howard, London: Jonathan Cape.

Baudrillard, Jean (1988) *America*, trans. Chris Turner, London: Verso.

—— (1995) *The Gulf War Did Not Take Place*, trans. Paul Patton, Sydney: Power Publications.

Beckett, Samuel (1994) *Malone Dies* in *Molloy, Malone Dies, The Unnamable*, London: Calder, pp. 177–289.

Belsey, Catherine (1999) *Shakespeare and the Loss of Eden: The Early Modern Construction of Family Values*, Basingstoke: Macmillan.

—— (2002a) *Critical Practice*, London: Routledge.

—— (2002b) *Poststructuralism: A Very Short Introduction*, Oxford: Oxford University Press.

Borch-Jacobsen, Mikkel (1991) *Lacan: The Absolute Master*, Stanford, CA: Stanford University Press.

—— (1999) 'Anna O.: The First Tall Tale', *Unauthorized Freud: Doubters Confront a Legend*, ed. Frederick Crews, Harmondsworth: Penguin, pp. 10–21.

Borges, Jorge Luis (1998) 'Tlön, Uqbar, Orbis Tertius', *Collected Fictions*, trans. Andrew Hurley, London: Allen Lane, pp. 68–81.

Bowie, Malcolm (1991) *Lacan*, London: Fontana.

Brown, Jonathan (1978) *Images and Ideas in Seventeenth-Century Spanish Painting*, Princeton, NJ: Princeton University Press.

—— and Carmen Garrido (1998) *Velázquez: the Technique of Genius*, New Haven and London: Yale University Press.

Butler, Judith (1993) *Bodies that Matter: On the Discursive Limits of 'Sex'*, New York: Routledge.

—— (1994) Peter Osborne and Lynne Segal, 'Gender as Performance: An Interview with Judith Butler', *Radical Philosophy* 67, 32–9.

—— (1997) *Excitable Speech: A Politics of the Performative*, New York: Routledge.

—— (1999) *Gender Trouble: Feminism and the Subversion of Identity*, second edition, New York: Routledge.

Damisch, Hubert (1994) *The Origin of Perspective*, trans. John Goodman, Cambridge, MA: MIT Press.

Deleuze, Gilles (1998) *Essays Critical and Clinical*, trans. Daniel W. Smith and Michael A. Greco, London: Verso.

Derrida, Jacques (1973) 'Differance', *'Speech and Phenomena' and Other Essays on Husserl's Theory of Signs*, trans. David B. Allison, Evanston, IL: Northwestern University Press, pp. 129–60.

—— (1987a) 'To Speculate – on "Freud"', *The Post Card: From Socrates to Freud and Beyond*, trans. Alan Bass, Chicago, IL: University of Chicago Press, pp. 257–409.

—— (1987b) *The Truth in Painting*, trans. Geoff Bennington and Ian McLeod, Chicago, IL: University of Chicago Press.

—— (1994) 'The Deconstruction of Actuality. An Interview with Jacques Derrida', *Radical Philosophy* 68 (Autumn), 28–41.

—— (2002) 'The Animal That Therefore I am (More to Follow)', trans. David Wills, *Critical Inquiry* 28, 369–418.

—— (2003) 'And Say the Animal Responded?', trans. David Wills, *Zoontologies: The Question of the Animal*, ed. Cary Wolfe, Minneapolis, MN: University of Minnesota Press, pp. 121–46.

Descartes, René (1988) *Selected Philosophical Writings*, trans. John Cottingham, Robert Stoothoff, Dugald Murdoch, Cambridge: Cambridge University Press.

Dickens, Charles (1996) *Bleak House*, ed. Nicola Bradbury, Harmondsworth: Penguin.

Duve, Thierry de (1999) *Kant After Duchamp*, Cambridge, MA: MIT Press.

Eagleton, Terry (1990) *The Ideology of the Aesthetic*, Oxford: Blackwell.

—— (2000) *The Idea of Culture*, Oxford: Blackwell.

Easthope, Antony (2002) *Privileging Difference*, Basingstoke: Palgrave-Macmillan.

Eliot, T. S. (1936) *Collected Poems, 1909–35*, London: Faber.

Evans, Dylan (1996) *An Introductory Dictionary of Lacanian Psychoanalysis*, London: Routledge.

Fink, Bruce (1995) *The Lacanian Subject: Between Language and Jouissance*, Princeton, NJ: Princeton University Press.

Fish, Stanley (1989) *Doing What Comes Naturally: Change, Rhetoric, and the Practice of Theory in Literary and Legal Studies*, Oxford: Clarendon Press.

Foucault, Michel (1970) *The Order of Things: An Archaeology of the Human Sciences*, London: Tavistock.

—— (1979) *The Will to Knowledge: The History of Sexuality, Volume One*, trans. Robert Hurley, London: Allen Lane.

Freud, Sigmund (1976) *Introductory Lectures on Psychoanalysis*, ed. James Strachey and Angela Richards, Harmondsworth: Penguin.

—— (1977a) *On Sexuality*, ed. Angela Richards, Harmondsworth: Penguin.

—— (1977b) *Case Histories I: 'Dora' and 'Little Hans'*, ed. Angela Richards, Harmondsworth: Penguin.

—— (1984) *On Metapsychology: The Theory of Psychoanalysis*, ed. Angela Richards, Harmondsworth: Penguin.

—— (1985a) *Civilization, Society and Religion*, ed. Albert Dickson, Harmondsworth: Penguin.

—— (1985b) 'The "Uncanny"', *Art and Literature*, ed. Albert Dickson, Harmondsworth: Penguin, pp. 335–76.

—— and Josef Breuer (1974) *Studies on Hysteria*, ed. Angela Richards, Harmondsworth: Penguin.

Hall, Edwin (1994) *The Arnolfini Bethrothal: Medieval Marriage and the Enigma of Van Eyck's Double Portrait*, Berkeley, CA: University of California Press.

Hegel, G. W. F. (1977) *Phenomenology of Spirit*, trans. A. V. Miller, Oxford: Oxford University Press.

Heidegger, Martin (1971) *Poetry, Language, Thought*, trans. Albert Hofstadter, New York: Harper & Rowe.

Jones, Ernest (1953) *Sigmund Freud: Life and Work*, vol. 1, London: Hogarth Press.

Joyce, James (1993) *Ulysses*, ed. Jeri Johnson, Oxford: Oxford University Press.

Justi, Carl [Karl] (1889) *Diego Velázquez and His Times*, trans. A. H. Keane, London: H. Grevel.

Kant, Immanuel (2000) *The Critique of the Power of Judgment*, trans. Paul Guyer and Eric Matthews, Cambridge: Cambridge University Press.

Kemp, Martin (1990) *The Science of Art: Optical Themes in Western Art from Brunelleschi to Seurat*, New Haven, CT: Yale University Press.

Lacan, Jacques (1973a) *Le Séminaire de Jacques Lacan, livre XI, Les Quatres concepts fondamentaux de la psychanalyse*, ed. Jacques-Alain Miller, Paris: Seuil.

—— (1973b) *Télévision*, Paris: Seuil.

—— (1975) *Le Séminaire de Jacques Lacan, livre XX, Encore*, ed. Jacques-Alain Miller, Paris: Seuil.

—— (1977) *Ecrits: A Selection*, trans. Alan Sheridan, London: Tavistock.

—— (1979) *The Four Fundamental Concepts of Psycho-analysis (Seminar 11)*, trans. Alan Sheridan, Harmondsworth: Penguin.

—— (1986) *Le Séminaire de Jacques Lacan, livre 7: L'éthique de la psychanalyse*, ed. Jacques-Alain Miller, Paris: Seuil.

—— (1988a) *Freud's Papers on Technique 1953–4 (Seminar 1)*, trans. John Forrester, Cambridge: Cambridge University Press.

—— (1988b) *The Ego in Freud's Theory and in the Technique of Psychoanalysis (Seminar 2)*, trans. Sylvana Tomaselli, Cambridge: Cambridge University Press.

—— (1990) *Television*, ed. Joan Copjec, New York: Norton.

—— (1992) *The Ethics of Psychoanalysis (Seminar 7)*, trans. Dennis Porter, London: Tavistock/Routledge.

—— (1998) *On Feminine Sexuality, the Limits of Love and Knowledge (Seminar 20)*, trans. Bruce Fink, New York: Norton.

Lyotard, Jean-François (1982) 'Réponse à la question: qu'est-ce que le postmoderne?', *Critique* 419 (April), 357–67.

—— (1984) *The Postmodern Condition: A Report on Knowledge*, trans. Geoff Bennington and Brian Massumi, Manchester: Manchester University Press.

—— (1991) *The Inhuman: Reflections on Time*, trans. Geoffrey Bennington and Rachel Bowlby, Cambridge: Polity Press.

—— (1994) *Lessons on the Analytic of the Sublime*, trans. Elizabeth Rottenberg, Stanford, CA: Stanford University Press.

—— (1997) *Postmodern Fables*, trans. Georges Van Den Abbeele, Minneapolis, MN: University of Minnesota Press.

Mallin, Eric S. (1999) '"You Kilt My Foddah": or Arnold, Prince of Denmark', *Shakespeare Quarterly* 50, 127–51.

Manetti, Antonio de Tuccio (1970) *The Life of Brunelleschi*, ed. Howard Saalman, University Park, PA: Pennsylvania State University Press.

Marvell, Andrew (1972) *The Complete Poems*, ed. Elizabeth Story Donno, Harmondsworth: Penguin.

Miller, Jonathan (1998) *On Reflection*, London: National Gallery.

Morrison, Toni (1987) *Beloved*, London: Chatto & Windus.

Palomino, Antonio (1987) *Lives of the Eminent Spanish Painters and Sculptors*, trans. Nina Ayala Mallory, Cambridge: Cambridge University Press.

Panofsky, Erwin (1953) *Early Netherlandish Painting: Its Origins and Character*, Cambridge, MA: Harvard University Press.

Pirandello, Luigi (2003) *Six Characters in Search of an Author*, trans. Stephen Mulrine, London: Nick Hern.

Readings, Bill (1991) *Introducing Lyotard: Art and Politics*, London: Routledge.

Rhys, Jean (1969) *Good Morning Midnight*, Harmondsworth: Penguin.

Saussure, Ferdinand de (1974) *Course in General Linguistics*, trans. Wade Baskin, London: Fontana.

Shakespeare, William (1997) *Sonnets*, ed. Katherine Duncan Jones. London: Nelson.

Shepherdson, Charles (2000) *Vital Signs: Nature, Culture, Psychoanalysis*, New York: Routledge.

Stoppard, Tom (1999) *Arcadia* in *Plays: 5*, London: Faber & Faber.

Thurber, James (1953) 'The Secret Life of Walter Mitty', *The Thurber Carnival*, Harmondsworth: Penguin, pp. 37–42.

Woolf, Virginia (1996) *Mrs Dalloway*, Harmondsworth: Penguin.

Žižek, Slavoj (1989) *The Sublime Object of Ideology*, London: Verso.

—— (1991) *Looking Awry: An Introduction to Lacan Through Popular Culture*, Cambridge, MA: MIT Press.

—— (1992a) *Enjoy Your Symptom! Jacques Lacan in Hollywood and Out*, New York: Routledge.

—— (1992b) *Everything You Always Wanted to Know About Lacan (But Were Afraid to Ask Hitchcock)*, London: Verso.

—— (1997) *The Plague of Fantasies*, London: Verso.

—— (1999a) *The Ticklish Subject: The Absent Centre of Political Ontology*, London: Verso.

—— (1999b) *The Žižek Reader*, ed. Elizabeth Wright and Edmond Wright, Oxford: Blackwell.

—— (2002) *Welcome to the Desert of the Real*, London: Verso.

INDEX

absolute 119–22, 124, 125, 127–8, 129–30, 138
aesthetics 120, 122–3, 125, 128, 129–30
Alberti, Leon Battista 90, 106, 110
Allen, Woody 1–2
Augustine 19, 107
Austen, Jane 82–6

Baby of Mâcon, The 6
Barnes, Julian 6–7
Barthes, Roland 41, 106, 119, 121–2
Baudrillard, Jean 3, 58–9
Beckett, Samuel 136, 152–5
Berkeley, Busby 135
Berkeley, George 63, 100–1
Borch-Jacobsen, Mikkel 34
Borges, Jorge Luis 20–1
Bosch, Hieronymus 55
Breuer, Josef 33
Brown, Jonathan 112–13

Brunelleschi, Filippo 87, 89–96, 103, 107, 110, 114–15, 133
Butler, Judith 4, 10–13, 15–16, 17, 19, 21, 24, 28–9, 63

Cabinet of Dr Caligari, The 135
Canaletto 96–9
Citizen Kane 136, 138
Claudel, Paul 73–4
Crivelli, Carlo 87–9, 92, 98
Cronenberg, David 8
Crosby, Bing 9
Cubism 131

Damisch, Hubert 90, 91, 93, 106, 115
Deleuze, Gilles 119, 122
Derrida, Jacques 45, 49–50, 59, 74, 94, 121
Descartes, René 15, 21, 24, 25–6, 32, 52, 100

Dickens, Charles 108–10, 114
Dubuffet, Jean 149
Duccio 86
Duchamp, Marcel 132–5, 137, 139
Duve, Thierry de 133, 149

Eagleton, Terry 10, 14, 124–5
Easthope, Antony 11
Eliot, T. S. 135
Emin, Tracey 132
epistemology 4, 22
eXistenZ 9
Eyck, Jan van 103–7, 115

Fish, Stanley 4, 15–16, 17, 19, 21,
    24, 63
Fontana, Lucio 149
Foucault, Michel 11, 12, 29, 113–14,
    143
foundationalism 10
Freud, Sigmund 5, 13, 19, 37, 62,
    63, 71, 102, 129–30, 147; 'Anna
    O.' 33–8; on death 41, 45–7;
    Little Ernst 47–8, 71, 73, 75; on
    sublimation 141, 143–5, 152; the
    'uncanny' 8–9; *see also*
    psychoanalysis

Giotto 86
Gogh, Vincent van 72–3, 76, 79
Graham-Dixon, Andrew 150
Greenblatt, Stephen 4

Habermas, Jürgen 125, 139
Hall, Edwin 103
Hegel, Georg Wilhelm Friedrich
    22–30, 53, 54, 56, 58, 61, 139
Heidegger, Martin 40, 54, 72–3,
    74
historicism 4, 23, 29, 63

Hobbes, Thomas 19
Hoogstraten, Samuel van 95–6
Hope, Bob 9
Hughes, Derek 79

Icicle Thief, The 6
idealism 15, 21–33, 52–63, 100–1,
    108, 118, 140

Johnson, Samuel 63
Joyce, James 135, 136
Judd, Donald 149
Justi, Karl 112, 115

Kabakov, Ilya and Emilia 149
Kant, Immanuel 22–3, 28–9, 53,
    54, 62, 125, 129–30, 139, 141;
    the beautiful 72–4, 120, 122,
    142; the sublime 119–30, 138,
    140, 141–2, 147, 148
Karloff, Boris 3
Kaye, Danny 2
Kemp, Martin 86, 91, 94, 110

Lacan, Jacques 4–6, 13–14, 18, 19,
    30–2, 39, 42, 49–50, 107, 114,
    117, 127, 129–30, 139–40, 152;
    Antigone 46, 57, 142–3, 146,
    147, 153; the beautiful 142–3,
    146, 148; culture 63, 65, 72–5,
    84, 85–6, 91, 147–8, 150, 155–6;
    death 40–1, 46–7, 57, 74,
    145–6; envy 107–8; 'Father,
    can't you see . . . ?' 5, 55–6;
    goods 71, 142, 146, 153; on
    idealism 61–3, 100; imaginary
    107, 125, 129; and Law 70–71;
    objet a 44–9, 52, 54, 55, 102,
    108, 118, 138; Other 5, 13, 14,
    30, 36, 47, 143; on sublimation

141–3, 145–6, 147–8, 155; the Thing (*das Ding*) 45, 47–9, 52, 54, 70–2, 84, 99, 102, 141, 142, 143, 145–6, 147, 152; and Žižek 5–6, 52–6, 57, 141–2, 147–8; *see also* psychoanalysis
Last Action Hero 7, 8
LeWitt, Sol 149
Locke, John 21–2
Lyotard, Jean-François 18, 119–20, 122, 125–32, 134–8, 139, 147, 148

McKellen, Ian 8
Manetti, Antonio 89–94
Man With a Movie Camera 135
Manzoni, Piero 132
Marvell, Andrew 42–4, 46
Marx Brothers 9
Matisse, Henri 131
meaning 4–5, 9, 13, 14, 15, 27, 30, 35–6, 41, 123
Miller, Jonathan 115
modernism 125–6, 127, 130, 131–2, 134–6, 148
Morrison, Toni 136, 138

Norris, Christopher 10

ontology 4, 22

Palomino, Antonio 110–12, 115
Panofsky, Erwin 103
Phiz (Hablôt K. Browne) 109–10, 114
Picasso, Pablo 117
Pirandello, Luigi 136
Plato 4, 10, 19, 127–8
Pleasantville 6
Pollock, Jackson 148–9

postmodernity 1–19, 119–20, 124–9, 130–2, 134–8, 139, 141
poststructuralism 4–6, 11, 12, 26, 139
psychoanalysis 5–6, 11, 13–14, 125, 129–30; the drive 13–14, 31, 37, 44–7, 50–51, 53, 54–6, 70–2, 75, 81, 84, 99, 144–6; the gaze 101–2; and paradox 38–42; and pleasure 71–2, 143, 147–8; resistance and 33–7; superego 144–6; *see also* Freud, Lacan
Purple Rose of Cairo, The 1–2, 6

resistance 16, 18–19, 29, 33–7, 156
Rhys, Jean 135
Rossetti, Dante Gabriel 131

Saussure, Ferdinand de 4, 13, 15, 41, 49, 127
Schwarzenegger, Arnold 7
Secret Life of Walter Mitty, The 2–3
Seventh Seal, The 8
Shakespeare, William 66, 77–9, 153
Shepherdson, Charles 32–3
Sheppard, John 65–7, 68–9, 75–7
Sickert, Walter 131
Simson, John 65–72, 75–80, 128
Sphere 55, 56
Stein, Gertrude 136
Stoppard, Tom 136, 138
surrealism 55
Swimming Pool 6

Thurber, James 3
Titian 102
Truman Show, The 16–17, 19

Ucello, Paolo 94

Velázquez, Diego 110–18
Vinci, Leonardo da 91, 94, 102, 106

Whistler, James 131
Whiteread, Rachel 150–2

Woolf, Virginia 135, 136

Žižek, Slavoj 5–6, 57, 60, 63;
idealism 52–6; the sublime
119–20, 139–42, 147–8

Critical Practice

Second Edition
Catherine Belsey
New Accents

'A fine assessment of recent work in literary theory and a
suggestive account of new directions for criticism to take.'

William E. Cain

What is poststructuralist theory, and what difference does it make
to literary criticism? Where do we find the meaning of the text:
in the author's head? in the reader's? Or do we, instead, *make* the
meaning in the practice of reading itself? If so, what part do our
own values play in the process of interpretation? And what is the
role of the text?

Catherine Belsey explains these and other questions concerning the
relations between human beings and language, readers and texts,
writing and cultural politics. The volume simply and lucidly explains
the views of such key figures as Louis Althusser, Roland Barthes,
Jacques Lacan and Jacques Derrida, and shows their theories at work
in readings of familiar literary texts.

With a new chapter, updated guidance on further reading and revi-
sions throughout, this second edition of *Critical Practice* is the ideal
guide to the present and the future of literary studies.

0-415-28005-2 (hbk)
0-415-28006-0 (pbk)

Available at all good bookshops

For ordering and further information please visit:
www.routledge.com